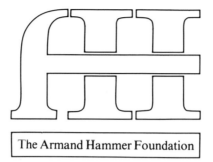

The Armand Hammer Foundation

The Armand Hammer Collection

Four Centuries of Masterpieces

Albright-Knox Art Gallery
Buffalo, New York

April 21 — May 29, 1978

Cover   REMBRANDT van Rijn (1606-1669)

Juno
Oil on canvas
50″ x 48 3/4″ (127.0 x 122.87 cm.)

4,000 copies printed for Albright-Knox Art Gallery

Table of Contents

Armand Hammer

THE ARMAND HAMMER FOUNDATION
10889 WILSHIRE BOULEVARD
LOS ANGELES, CALIFORNIA 90024

Collecting art is a challenge, one I have pursued throughout my life. Traveling the world over I have seen that art has a universal way of speaking to each one of us, allowing us to look at ourselves with greater insight, enabling us to see people of other times and places, providing us with a unique opportunity to share a common bond of wonder and delight.

What you see before you is my attempt over many years to assemble and chronicle some of the visions of man's realities and dreams brought forth by artistic genius. All that I earnestly hope for is that we shall share these visions and the joys of the artists represented in this Collection in an era of peace and prosperity.

With this spirit and with this wish, I should like to greet you and bid you welcome. I feel honored that the Albright-Knox Art Gallery has selected The Armand Hammer Collection for exhibition.

Sincerely,

Armand Hammer

Armand Hammer

Preface

Why do men collect works of art? What motivations encourage the development of the connoisseur, the collector, and the patron of the arts like the extraordinary interests of Dr. Armand Hammer over the past several decades?

Sure answers universally applicable will probably never be found to questions concerning a human activity almost as old as recorded history. But some observations may be helpful in seeking to understand this special characteristic of man.

One of the basic goals, of course, is the aesthetic enjoyment that works of art bring. This simple elusive pleasure, it seems to me, is often obscured by the complex layers of analysis laid upon the character and circumstances of those motivated to collect by others not bitten by the same bug, yet determined to find out what there is to it. Perhaps it amounts to, as well, something Saint-Exupéry decribed in explaining why young men took such terrible chances as pilots flying flimsy aircraft over dangerous, long-distance ocean routes -- the emotion he described as "le désire à toucher la grandeur." Not only can fine works of art bring pleasure but they can give one the sense, by involvement with them, of participating in a universal movement of some kind.

Universal? Does anything, after all, penetrate cultural, historical and national barriers as effectively as art? How basic is art?

The anthropologist, Claude Lévi-Strauss states quite simply that art is the one "fundamental" form of knowledge in human experience.

If, like the aesthete, fish divide perfumes into light and dark, and bees classify luminosity in terms of weight...the work of the painter, the poet, or the musician, like the myths and symbols of the savage, ought to be seen by us, if not as a superior form of knowledge, at least as the most fundamental and the only one really common to us all. [1]

He continues to comment that in contrast to art, which is the widest type of human perception, "scientific thought is merely the sharp point" of the tool of knowledge, "more penetrating because it has been whetted on the stone of fact, but at the cost of some loss of substance..." [2]

In modern times, the greatest collectors have instinctively understood the public nature of art and have underscored its universal appeal by supporting art institutions and their activities. Few have reached the level of commitment and achievement that Dr. Armand Hammer has. His collection, which is documented in this catalogue, has been viewed by millions of people on four continents over the past ten years.

Dr. Hammer's personal brand of diplomacy in Moscow, where he is the best-known American from the private sector, resulted in the series of impressive exhibitions of Soviet State-owned treasures from the museums of Moscow, Leningrad and Kiev in this country. In his own view, which is obviously a tremendously successful one, art is, in fact, an "emissary" bound to recall as well the observation of Lévi-Strauss that art is the most fundamental form of knowledge and communication.

It is a privilege and honor to present these 109 works of art at the Albright-Knox Art Gallery, ranging over four centuries of achievement and representing seven cultures. Seymour H. Knox, Chairman of the Board of Directors of The Buffalo Fine Arts Academy, joins me in expressing sincere gratitude to Dr. Hammer for the generous loan of his collection for exhibition in Buffalo. I wish to thank Olga Hammer, Director of Art/Curator of The Armand Hammer Foundation, who has aided us in every step of this project. I further wish to acknowledge the support of the Hooker Chemical Corporation for this project. John S. Coey, President; John J. Lenahan, Executive Vice President; and Charles Y. Cain, Vice President for Corporate Affairs, who originally suggested the possibility of bringing the collection to Buffalo, have been helpful from the start. James M. Green, Manager of Public Relations, has effectively served as corporate liaison for this project. Finally, the Gallery staff in general and especially Douglas G. Schultz, Curator in charge of the installation; Serena Rattazzi, Coordinator of Public Relations; Karen Spaulding, Editor of Publications; Jane E. Nitterauer, Registrar; and John J. Kushner, Superintendent of the Building, have devoted many hours to making the most effective presentation of these rare and beautiful objects in the Gallery possible.

Robert T. Buck, Jr.
Director, Albright-Knox Art Gallery

1 Claude Lévi-Strauss, *Tristes tropiques*, Atheneum, New York 1975, p. 123.
2 Ibid.

Introduction

I once asked Armand Hammer why he collected. "Because it's fun!" he explained. "It's a hunt. I get a certain joy out of finding rare works, out of learning the stories attached to them. I've always liked to collect. I used to collect stamps. My father had a great stamp collection. But pictures are something more than just collecting. You are connecting yourself with something that really is immortal, something that has survived all these centuries. You are preserving something for posterity".

Armand Hammer is a doctor of medicine although he has never practiced. He received his degree from the Columbia Medical School, studying at night and in the daytime running a family pharmaceutical company. The family firm was on the verge of bankruptcy, but he made it so profitable that on graduation he had a clear profit of one million dollars.

While waiting to begin his internship at the Bellevue Medical Center, he decided in 1921 to go to Russia whence his grandfather had emigrated, and to use his medical knowledge and a field hospital he had purchased to combat typhus, which was raging in the Urals. He found, however, when after many difficulties he got to the Russian interior, that though typhus was everywhere, the real enemy was starvation. The famine he saw struck him, as he said, "with cold horror". He decided to use a substantial part of his capital to eliminate the terrible shortage of food. He entered into an agreement with the local Soviet that he buy a million bushels of American wheat, which he estimated would feed the local population until their own crops, destroyed by a combination of drought and Revolution, were once more harvestable. He stipulated, however, that the ships bringing the grain be filled with Russian goods which could be sold in the United States, so that the food supply could be replenished.

When Lenin heard of this, he asked to meet this young American, who at twenty-three had become a hero in the Urals. The meeting between the two was an immediate success. They became and remained firm friends. Lenin proposed that Armand Hammer accept one or more Soviet concessions. After thinking over the offer, he decided to choose two, one for mining asbestos, which proved minimally profitable, and the

second for an export-import business, which succeeded beyond his most sanguine hopes. He represented eventually thirty-seven leading American companies, and he was the first to import Fordson tractors, thus beginning the mechanization of Russian agriculture.

He settled down in Moscow and spent the next nine years in the Soviet Union. Needing a residence, he rented an unfurnished palace, and decorating it gave him his first interest in art. His younger brother, Victor, who had studied art history at Princeton, became Armand's tutor. Together they bought, for next to nothing, Eighteenth-Century French furniture, Aubusson rugs, services of Sévres china, Meissen porcelains, all the household furnishings which were sold in Commission Stores where such treasures were brought by the impoverished aristocracy and even the middle class.

Around 1928 a New York art dealer, seeing the bargains the Hammer brothers were picking up, offered a partnership in his firm, and Victor joined his company. Armand soon bought out the other partner, who had been ruined in the stock market collapse, and the Hammer Galleries were established. Meanwhile the Hammer palace in Moscow rivalled any museum of decorative arts, and their acquisitions also filled several warehouses. Having paid a tax to the Soviets, they were allowed to export these treasures, and this became the stock which Armand and Victor brilliantly sold in the Hammer Galleries over a period of years. This, the first Hammer Collection, has all been dispersed. It was essentially a way of converting rubles into dollars.

Thus for a long time art dealing has been the avocation of Armand Hammer. He is the President of Hammer Galleries as well as President of M. Knoedler and Co., Inc. Victor is the active manager of the Hammer Galleries. But Armand's real vocation has been a search for still more rewarding enterprises. In Russia, apart from his export-import business, he built and operated a pencil factory which at its peak produced seventy-two million pencils and ninety-five million pens a year and made a tremendous profit. Departing from Russia in 1930, he ran a private bank in Paris, which specialized in discounting Soviet notes at twenty-four per cent per annum, holding them until they were paid in full, and often making as much as seventy per cent on each transaction. He then returned to America and, after having sold most of his Russian collection, helped liquidate the Hearst works of art.

During World War II he built the first distillery in this country to make alcohol from potatoes; and substituting potato spirits for grain spirits, which were embargoed, he developed a valuable business in blended whiskey. After the war he bought several other distilleries which used the more conventional grain alcohol. In a few years he built the J. W. Dant brand from a relatively unknown Kentucky bourbon into a company selling over a million cases a year. In 1954 he finally sold this whiskey empire to Schenley Distillers and moved to California. But his most successful venture was his investment in Occidental Petroleum Corporation, of which he has been President and is now Chairman and Chief Executive Officer. To give some idea of the growth of this company under his leadership, in 1956, when he first became associated with it, its total assets were under forty thousand dollars; today they are five and one-third billion dollars.

Occidental Petroleum has made possible the third Hammer Collection. For there was a second Hammer Collection formed in the fifties and given to the University of Southern California in 1965. These paintings constitute an important group of Old Masters intended for study purposes and have proved invaluable in a university museum. But when he had given them away, Dr. Hammer began a more ambitious collection with a particular emphasis on French Impressionists, Post-Impressionists, and Old Master paintings and drawings. This, the third Hammer Collection, is illustrated and annotated in the present catalog. Today this exceptional group of paintings and drawings contains more than 100 masterpieces that span four centuries of western European and American works including those of Leonardo da Vinci, Michelangelo, Picasso and Chagall.

The uniqueness and quality of these valuable art works are evident in the paintings of the period extending from the Sixteenth to the Twentieth Century. The "crown jewel" of the collection is the *Juno* by Rembrandt once owned by William Middendorf.

I recall how this supremely beautiful work struck me as unsurpassed among its greatest peers when I first saw it exhibited. It is, in my opinion, the finest single work of art which has remained in an American private collection. Like the drawing by Leonardo, it too is a memory image — a loving tribute to Hendrickje Stoffels, Rembrandt's mistress, who died in 1663, probably the year the canvas was begun. Dr. Hammer has said that he acquired the painting with the intention of presenting it to the Los Angeles County Museum. In the rapidly growing collection of that remarkable gallery, the Rembrandt *Juno* will long remain its outstanding treasure and also a magnet of visitors to the museum.

Though the focus is on paintings of the Nineteenth-and-Twentieth Centuries, the works of several earlier masters are represented. The Los Angeles County Museum of Art was enabled by the Armand and Frances Hammer Purchase Fund to acquire two splendid Seventeenth-Century panels: Rembrandt's *Portrait of a Man of the Raman Family* and Rubens' *The Israelites Gathering Manna in the Desert.* A second Rubens in the Hammer Collection, *Young Woman with Curly Hair,* is particularly distinguished for its flesh tones, as beautiful as any I know in painting, and for its modeling, breathtaking in the subtlety of the transitions of shadow.

There are only two Eighteenth-Century paintings in the exhibition. The first, Fragonard's *The Education of the Virgin,* owes its chiaroscuro and sepia tones to Rembrandt and its fluent brushwork and virtuosity to Rubens. Dr. Hammer was fortunate enough to acquire for the collection the preliminary sketch for this beautiful painting. The second, a sketch by Goya, *El Pelele,* for the Prado cartoon, was selected by the Spanish Society of the Friends of Art for their exhibition of Goya's work in Madrid, a fact worth noting, since the finest Spanish pictures meet their exacting standards.

Corot has always been for Armand Hammer a favorite artist. At one time there were twenty-four of his paintings in the collection. Of these only the six finest are being shown. Historically the most interesting is a landscape known as *Pleasures of Evening,* an appropriate title for it is one of the artist's last canvases. Writing about it in 1892, Castagnary touchingly said, "When the imagination is still so fresh, and sensitivity still so alive, death should take pity and not interrupt". The painting has darkened with time, as happens often with Corot's late work. Thus there will always be those who prefer the fresh, spring-like tones of *Distant View of Mantes Cathedral.* For my part I would choose the dramatic *Medieval Ruins,* or, among figure pictures, the portrait of a young minx *(Portrait of a Girl)* whose half-smile and appraising glance enthrall me.

With Corot as its leader, the greatest school of landscape painting the world has known, even without the geniuses of Constable and Turner, flourished in and around Paris. To realize this one need only look at Boudin, whose mastery of cloud effects is impressively demonstrated by *Sailing Ships in Port;* at Renoir, whose infectious *joie de vivre* is gloriously apparent both in *Grape Pickers at Lunch,* an enchanting peasant picnic, and in *Antibes,* which suggests a modern *Embarkation for Cythera;* and at Monet whose palette, in that masterpiece of light and air, *View of Bordighera,* seems made of ground jewels. All these paintings illustrate the reason for the popularlity of the Impressionists and their circle. One of the most enchanting cityscapes ever painted, Pissarro's *Boulevard Montmartre, Mardi Gras,* which recently moved from one California collector to another, from Norton Simon to Armand Hammer, shows the quintessence of this Impressionist technique. It vibrates with light and color, an effect only possible through the use of those quick, short brush strokes which are the hallmark of Impressionism.

There was, of course, the reaction against the Impressionists, exemplified by Cézanne, van Gogh and Gauguin. All these artists are well represented in the Hammer Collection. The Cézanne *Boy Resting* has been frequently exhibited; the Gauguin *Bonjour M. Gauguin,* a later version of which is in Prague, has been widely reproduced; and the four van Goghs, *Garden of Rectory at Neunen,* an early work, *The Sower,* somewhat later and obviously influenced by Millet, *Lilacs,* a still life seemingly redolent of the fragrance of lilacs, and *Hospital at Saint Rémy,* where van Gogh was confined, are all well known. The latter, once in the Norton Simon Collection, is one of van Gogh's supreme works. Of this view of the park and the asylum he wrote, "I tried to reconstruct the thing as it might have been, simplifying and accentuating the haughty, unchanging character of the pines and cedar clumps against the blue".

American collectors have been so preoccupied with the Impressionists and their followers that there has been a tendency to overlook artists who did not belong to the movement. Among these to me the most enthralling is Gustave Moreau, who was a direct precursor of the Surrealists. Armand Hammer owns two of his masterpieces, *King David* and *Salome.* The latter had a deep effect on J. K. Huysman, and in *A Rebours* he wrote a long description of the picture in prose as glittering as the painting itself. In 1876 P. de Saint-Victor said of it: "M. Gustave Moreau's entry in the Salon far exceeds any of his previous exhibits....If an opium fiend could translate his visions into reality with a goldsmith's skill, it would give some idea of this artist".

Another French artist less collected than he deserves to be is Fantin-Latour. His still lifes of flowers are often to be found in American collections, though never in a finer example than Dr. Hammer's *Peonies in a Blue and White Vase,* but his superb portraits are too rarely seen. *Portrait of Miss Edith Crowe* is one of the most poetic examples of Nineteenth-Century portraiture. The strongly accented light and shadow create a mood of pensive brooding, the essence of the Romantic image.

The momentum of the great French artistic movements of the Nineteenth-Century carried creativity well into the first half of the Twentieth-Century. The artists who made Paris in our time the mecca for painters, especially Vuillard and Bonnard, are beautifully shown. It is difficult to choose among the Vuillards, they are all of such high quality. But my favorite remains *At the Seashore.* Jacques Salomon in a recent book perfectly expresses my response to this exquisite canvas when he says it "is like a cry from the heart, the echo of which ravished me...the touch is so alive, so alert, so completely submissive to the rhythm of Vuillard's feeling".

Bonnard, too, is well represented. The early *Street Scene* evokes the loveliness of the simplest happenings of Parisian life, and the *Nude Against the Light* suggests the artist's unique combination of sensitivity and sensuality, reminding one of the nudes Titian painted at the end of his life.

The next generation which lends such lustre to the School of Paris is to be seen in a great portrait by Modigliani, already a part of the collection of the Los Angeles County Museum of Art; by Vlaminck's *Summer Bouquet,* equaling de Staël in its display of palette knife virtuosity: and by Derain's *Still Life with Basket, Jug and Fruit* which is distinguished for its simplicity of composition, its elimination to essential forms, and its restricted palette.

I have kept to the last, two paintings, both as insubstantial as a dream: Marie Laurencin's *Women in the Forest,* which once belonged to John Quinn, the pioneer among American collectors in his appreciation of the School of Paris; and Chagall's *Blue Angel,* which was once in the collection of Frank Crowinshield, the able editor of *Vanity Fair,* a publication largely responsible for the American vogue of these Parisian artists.

In recent years Dr. Hammer has added to his collection several American paintings. His earliest picture is the most famous of American icons, Gilbert Stuart's *Portrait of George Washington.* Known as the *Lewis Washington,* it is more interesting than many other versions, showing the first President seated at a table with his sword resting on his arm and a glimpse of sky in the distance.

A great portrait painted just eighty years later is Thomas Eakins' *Sebastiano Cardinal Martinelli.* In its psychological penetration, its simplicity and dignity, its noble humanity, this may well be considered an American Rembrandt. Sylvan Schendler, writing in 1967, refers to it as "the most powerful portrait of its kind ever painted by an American".

Slightly earlier is a fine still life by Harnett, which has the distinction of being among the few Nineteenth-Century American pictures ever exhibited at the Royal Academy, where it was shown in 1885 and bought by an English painter, George Richmond.

The American canvas, *On the Beach,* painted in 1916 by Maurice Prendergast, is the most original and interesting American Impressionist. Owned by Mrs. Charles Prendergast until recently, it is a picture she parted with reluctantly as it was always considered in the family one of her brother-in-law's greatest masterpieces.

Two Americans who lived abroad, Mary Cassatt and John Singer Sargent, are superbly represented, each by two pictures, one of the Sargents having been bought by the Los Angeles County Museum of Art with funds provided by Dr. and Mrs. Hammer. Mary Cassatt's double portrait of *Reine Lefebvre and Margot* is, in my opinion, her finest pastel done after 1900, and the idyllic *Summertime* I consider one of her two most important landscapes.

The two portraits by Sargent, though both were painted relatively early, are totally different from each other. *Dr. Pozzi at Home,* dated 1881, is highly dramatic, as though the doctor were an actor about to go on stage. It is a masterpiece of Salon painting, sophisticated and cosmopolitan. The double portrait of *Mrs. Edward L. Davis and Her Son, Livingston Davis,* is much more sober, more American in a straightforward, realistic way. Sargent has here recorded the essence of upper class America, which has learned to be fashionable without learning to be chic.

I have already mentioned a few of the drawings owned by Dr. Hammer. In recent years this part of his collection has been greatly enriched and he has collected the most important privately owned collection of drawings in America. Several of his finest acquisitions have been made in 1970 and 1971. These begin with a lovely watercolor of flowers by Albrecht Dürer, a study by Raphael for S. Maria della Pace in Rome, and two studies by Correggio, one for the pendentive of San Giovanni Evangelista in Parma and the other for the Madonna della Scodella, both published in 1970 by Oberhuber.

But the two most important drawings recently added to the Hammer Collection are by the two most important of all Renaissance artists: Leonardo da Vinci and Michelangelo. These studies rank with the finest examples of the graphic arts ever brought to America.

The Leonardo is probably a fragment of a large sheet, which must have been the size of the drawing of the *Virgin, Christ Child, and St. John* at Windsor, generally dated 1478-80. The ink and paper are the same, and, for the following reasons, it seems to have been done at about the same time. At the bottom of the sheet there is a bust of a young girl who looks at the spectator. She closely resembles a drawing by Leonardo at Oxford of a maiden with a unicorn. Some years ago in an article on Leonardo's *Ginerva dei Benci* I pointed out the similarity of the Oxford sketch and the portrait, which I date about 1480, or in exactly the same period as the Windsor sheet. Fortunately Dr. Hammer has indicated that his drawings will go to Washington, and thus the National Gallery of Art will some day have not only Ginerva's actual portrait but what might be called a memory image of her face, a tracing of that strange beauty which haunted the master's mind in his youth, in the days just after he had gained his independence from his apprenticeship with Verrocchio.

Michelangelo's drawing in black chalk, recto-verso, of two nude men both leaning forward may be, as tentatively suggested by John Gere and Nicholas Turner, the germ of the concept of his greatest of all *Pietas,* the one once owned by the Rondanini family. All the contours of the figures, especially the outlines of each side of the torsos and limbs, are so sensitively related one to the other that they suggest three-dimensional forms as weighty and solid as the marble from which the *Pieta* was carved. It is further believed to be the studies for the figures of the Epifania cartoon.

Another discovery is a biblical subject by Rembrandt in the process of being published by Christopher White. Also recently added is a brown ink *Study of a Beggar Man and Woman* done about 1630 that displays Rembrandt's fascination with life in Amsterdam.

At the sale of Mrs. Jesse I. Strauss' fastidiously chosen collection he bought two exquisite Eighteenth-Century sanguines by Watteau, four virtuoso performances in sepia wash by Fragonard, a serenely beautiful pencil portrait of *Mrs. Badham* drawn by Ingres when he was in Rome, and the fascinating Degas pastel of *Jacquet,* whose staring eyes are so strangely hypnotic.

From the Norton Simon sale he acquired two Boucher drawings, one *Venus Reclining Against a Dolphin,* which was engraved by Demarteau, and the other, *Landscape,* which was selected by Agnes Mongan for *Great Drawings of All Times.*

A drawing by Daumier in watercolor, ink and wash of a lawyer pleading for his client, ranks among the artist's finest achievements. The old bespectacled advocate is vibrant with passion, and the whole court seems caught up in the intensity of the drama. One is almost overwhelmed by the concentrated endeavor of the unknown lawyer. A second drawing is a preliminary sketch for the *Third Class Carriage.*

The drawings in Dr. Hammer's collection range from the shorthand annotations of the artist's immediate response to nature in the Gauguin *Sketchbook* to Ingres' portrait of *Mrs. Badham,* fashioned as a complete and independent work of art. Ingres' idealism based on nature is a concept of art which extends back through artists and writers of the intervening centuries to the Renaissance, with Raphael as its model. It is this concept that the leaders of the major movements in Nineteenth-Century art attacked again and again, but to which they often returned for sustenance. The drawings in the Hammer Collection could, in fact, be viewed as a dialectic between Ingres and the other artists represented here who effected the transition in concept, style and subject from the art of the Old Masters to modern art.

Working for the open market without ecclesiastical or aristocratic commissions, the artists of the Nineteenth Century had the freedom to adhere to the precepts of the Academy or to seek independent subjects, styles and livelihoods. The result was that the creative personalities produced a series of revolutions and counter-revolutions in rapid succession paralleling the extraordinary social and intellectual developments of the century. Their unifying element was the study of the Old Masters and the respect for Ingres whose influence persists in drawings of Manet, Degas, Renoir and Seurat.

The artists working in the middle of the century, represented here by Millet and Daumier, turned first to the landscape and the peasant and eventually to the urban poor and middle class. In the Ingres portrait, the human figure so dominates its surrounding that even as grandiose an environment as the city of Rome becomes a stage set for the sitter; in the Millet pastel, the peasants are an integral part of the landscape, sharing their reality with the cart and tree and the undulations of the land. The thick line and broad surface modulations give weight and solidity to the peasant figures but, at the same time, imbue them with a simple dignity that goes back in French tradition beyond the writings of Jean Jacques Rousseau to the nobility of the peasants in the painting of Louis LeNain.

Possibly no group of artists who exhibited together and consequently received a single art historical label are more divergent than the Impressionists. Descended from the mid-century painters of reality, the Impressionists in the 1860's and 1870's espoused the common aim of depicting nature through the color and light perceived by the eye, rather than through tangible forms recreated by the intellect. In drawing they achieved this end by softening outlines, varying the width and intensity of strokes to suggest value gradations of color, using the spare areas of the paper to enhance the illusion of light and atmosphere and replacing traditional linear perspective with aerial perspective. The drawings, watercolors and pastels in the Hammer Collection by Pissarro, Manet, Degas and Renoir reveal such highly individualized perceptions of "optical reality" and such different moments in the history of Impressionism that they are best considered as works by individual Impressionist artists rather than as representative of a unified Impressionist style.

Millet insisted that he was completely apolitical, while Camille Pissarro was an anarchist with Marxian sympathies and a strong identification with the underprivileged. Yet Pissarro's representation of peasants in the *Pea Harvest* certainly influenced by Millet, is neither polemic nor sentimental; it is rather a reflection of the Impressionist view of the subject as an essentially pictorial element. Pissarro's particular concern for the peasants is implied in his choice of them as subjects, otherwise rare in Impressionist art, and he rendered them without movement, standing or kneeling, almost immobile as though the artist wished

to record their forms silhouetted against a blank background as images of timelessness. *Montmorency Road,* drawn with the utmost restraint and delicacy, is a characteristic example of Pissarro's landscape style in the medium of pencil. Here the Impressionist artist has abstracted the generalized forms of the objects, reducing them to the basic realities of light and shade.

Edouard Manet in his early double-sided charcoal drawing of a *Man Wearing a Cloak* adapted the grandiose concept of the figure and the use of chiaroscuro to suggest fluid mass rather than modeled volumes from another source, the drawings of the Baroque masters, some of whom he was later to accept as his antecedents in "pure painting".

In his book, *The Nude,* Kenneth Clark wrote that Edgar Degas "was the greatest draughtsman since the Renaissance. His subject was the figure in action, his aim to communicate most vividly the idea of movement." This statement immediately conjures up the image of one of Degas' lithe ballerinas caught in a graceful arabesque on a brilliantly lighted stage. It applies equally to the figurative pastels of the 1880's in the Hammer Collection when Degas had abandoned spontaneous action and conventional beauty of figure and setting. The *Laundress Carrying Linen,* a descendant of Daumier's working women, but for Degas without social implications, is a "figure in action" in a Poussinesque sense embodying the tensions created by the weight of the laundry and the counteracting torsions of the figure.

The *Theater Box* captures the kaleidoscopic movement of members of the corps-de-ballet in an instantaneous pattern and gives it permanency. Experimenting with artificial illumination, Degas shrouds a large part of the composition in darkness and shadows. The cropped silhouettes emphasize the fragmented figures on stage caught in fleeting gestures and rapid complex movements. Painted about 1885, it heralds both Expressionism and abstract art.

Pierre Renoir, along with Monet the purest Impressionist of the 1870's, also experienced the crisis in that style after his trip to Italy in 1881. His pencil drawing in the Hammer Collection of two seated girls in *Girlhood* seen from behind still has something of the casualness and colorism of Impressionism. The figures are not defined by a firm sculptural line like that of Ingres but by fragile strokes of varied width and darkness which suggest atmosphere surrounding the figures and playing over the surfaces. Yet, in this drawing the artist self-consciously transcends purely optical vision to suggest the stability of form beneath the surface.

Discovering and recording the underlying forms and structures of that bright and sunny nature revealed by the Impressionists became the artistic preoccupation of Cézanne and the Neo-Impressionists. Cézanne spoke of making of Impressionism "something solid and durable like the art of the museums." Towards this end he made studies like that in the Hammer Collection of a plaster cast of a male figure with the skin removed to reveal the muscles, a cast thought at that time to be by Michelangelo. He injected into it the kind of energy welling up from within the figure that was not likely present in the cast itself. The reverse side has been described by John Rewald as a "study" for the painting *The Artist's Father* at the National Gallery of Art in Washington D. C. To quote Rewald: "While contemplating him, often without the model's knowledge, the painter had felt the deep-rooted links that nature or fate had established between him and this old man."

The Neo-Impressionists followed Georges Seurat whose goal was a scientific, objective and non-individualist system for depicting the essential reality of nature. He strived to capture this quality in his carefully controlled space of the *Study after 'The Models'*. Despite the brevity of Seurat's career, a prodigious body of drawings celebrates his genius as a draftsman. Curiously, among the several hundred drawings assigned to his hand, only two were intended by the artist to be graphically reproduced. The present drawing derives from one of Seurat's major canvases, *The Models,* and was used for an illustration in April 15, 1888 issue of *La Vie Moderne.* In the following year, Seurat designed a cover for *L'Homme a Femme,* a novel by the Polish writer, Victor Joze. Each of these studies was drawn in pen and ink, a technique that rarely appears in Seurat's drawing oeuvre. Another

atypical feature common to both is the undisguised use of outline.

Henri-Edmond Cross' *Cypresses* with its feeling of romantic nostalgia, is clear evidence that Neo-Impressionist style and technique in other hands could be used as a vehicle for extra-pictorial emotional communication.

The last direct derivation from Impressionism in the Hammer Collection is the delicate and poetic *Girl Drying Her Knees* by Pierre Bonnard who continued working in this manner into the fifth decade of the Twentieth-Century. The present work is one of the most freely executed of these sketches, done with great economy of lines. It evokes a sense of freedom and, at the same time, a springy feeling of movement which is rather infrequent in Bonnard's generally motionless figure studies.

The Hammer Collection is richest in the early drawings of the two artists Vincent van Gogh and Paul Gauguin, who led the way from Impressionism to personal emotional expression and laid the basis for the Expressionism of the Twentieth-Century. The two drawings of houses by van Gogh are among his very earliest serious works dated 1879-1880. He had made drawings from childhood and had been associated with works of art during his entire life through his three brothers who were art dealers and his own occupation as an assistant at Goupil & Co. for seven years. It was only after his dismissal from this position and his failure as an evangelist among the poor miners in the Borinage district of Belgium that he, still living among the poor workers, decided to become an artist. It was then in early 1880 that these simple charcoal studies of houses were made. There are already hints here of that nervous line which gave such vitality to his later works. Van Gogh quickly transferred his evangelical commisseration with the poor to drawing workmen and peasants. The drawings of the two old men of 1882, one of a *Man Polishing a Boot* and the *Old Man Carrying a Bucket,* are executed in what can be called van Gogh's first personal style; rather bulky figures, tight and angular with a rich elaboration of surface. These four drawings furnish a revealing contrast to his subsequent progress. During this period he made scores of drawings after Millet and studied for fifteen months with Anton Mauve. The growth of the artist between 1882 and 1884, when the watercolor *The Weaver* was painted, is extraordinary. The forms are more fluid, the transitions easier, and the perspective more natural. But for van Gogh, the technique was only the means of depicting the mechanized weaver enslaved as he described to his brother to "that black colossus of dirty oak with all its sticks" which he must manipulate "from early to late... they are but poor creatures, those weavers." Dr. Hammer has just recently given this work to the Louvre Museum - Cabinet of Drawings at the opening of The Armand Hammer Nineteenth-Century Drawing Collection.

Of singular historical importance is a sketchbook of Paul Gauguin which has been disassembled for purposes of exhibition. Gauguin purchased the sketchbook in Rouen in 1884 and used it intermittently until 1888. It includes brief lists, shopping lists, addresses and notations which clarify events in Gauguin's life during those years. Eleven pages concern Gauguin's thoughts on art, *Notes Synthetiques* his first written statement on art theory as well as notes on literature and music. The remaining 105 pages are filled with 268 sketches of landscapes, houses, animals and people mostly from Brittany; many of the images used in pictures of the same period. The color crayon drawings of the *Breton Boy,* typical of Gauguin's style, in the sketchbook show that at that time the artist was still closely linked to Impressionism. The poses are informal, casual with few details. The forms dissolve in transparent etchings of light tones while other drawings clearly anticipate the arbitrary flat pattern and calligraphic line of the *Landscape at Pont-Aven* or the primitive simplification of *Parau No Te Varau Ino* which characterizes the later Gauguin. The *Gauguin Sketchbook,* Dr. Hammer has said "is for me like being taken into the mind of the artist. It is the extension of the artist as he responds to life and records it. These drawings give insight to the creative processes."

Talking to Armand Hammer, one feels the intense intellectual concentration which enables him to develop solutions for problems and issues confronting him, whether in his youth it involved the pharmaceutical company or Russian famine, or later the sale of Fordson tractors or the manufacture of lead pencils, or after his Russian sojourn the dispersal of his first art collection or the distilling of whiskey, or today the development of Occcidental Petroleum Corporation, or the search for a cure for cancer through the Armand Hammer Center for Cancer Research at Salk Institute in La Jolla, California, or the Julius and Armand Hammer Health Sciences Center at Columbia University which is their alma mater. Not the least of his endeavors is the assembling of the present collection of works of art for the benefit of the public. The paintings will ultimately hang in the Frances and Armand Hammer Wing of the Los Angeles County Museum of Art and the drawings are destined to hang in the National Gallery of Art.

Armand Hammer is not like other collectors. His delight is in the quest, not the possession. None of his great paintings or drawings hang in his house. He is satisfied to live with a fine copy by Mrs. Hammer of the Modigliani portrait bought with his funds by the Los Angeles County Museum of Art, and with a few Impressionist paintings of slight importance. At seventy-nine he works as hard as anyone I have ever known. Much of his life is spent in his airplane flying from one place to another, tirelessly seeking to improve the earnings of Occidental Petroleum. He feels a deep sense of obligation to the shareholders, but he is also interested in making money himself. Why? For the sheer joy of giving it away. It may or may not be true that it is more blessed to give than to receive. But Armand Hammer would say it is certainly much more fun!

John Walker

Director Emeritus, National Gallery of Art, Washington, D.C.

Acknowledgments

Dr. Armand Hammer is a world citizen in his business life, a world resident in his private life. His philosophy of art and his sense of trusteeship as a collector are equally international in perspective. "A drawing by Rembrandt or a painting by van Gogh doesn't communicate only in Dutch," Dr. Hammer observes, "it speaks in English, French, Spanish, Russian, Japanese, and in as many other languages as there are viewers." For him, the work of art transcends not only linguistic barriers but the limits of language itself in expressing many subtleties of human experience and human perception which cannot be formulated in words. It is, therefore, an ideal vehicle not only for giving visual pleasures to people wherever they might live but also for expanding their understanding of man both individually as a feeling and thinking being and commonly as part of the diverse social and cultural complexes he has created. The collection that Dr. Hammer assembled is one of considerable variety, extending from the Renaissance into the first decades of the 20th century, having as its unifying constituent the representation of man and nature. It includes works of artists like Rembrandt, Daumier and van Gogh deeply concerned with human psychology and condition; of others like the French realists and most of the Americans intent upon recording their personal visions of nature; and of still others who extract elements from nature to be savored aesthetically: color for the Impressionists, form for Cézanne and Seurat.

In keeping with his belief in the importance of works of art as vehicles of pleasure and understanding, Dr. Hammer has a deeply felt commitment to sharing his collection. Consequently, no other private collection has been seen in recent times by so many people in such different parts of the world. In 1972 it was exhibited at the Royal Academy of Arts in London and the National Gallery of Ireland in Dublin; in 1972-3 at the Hermitage Museum in Leningrad, the Pushkin Museum in Moscow, the State Museum of Fine Arts of the Ukranian Socialist Soviet Republic in Kiev, the State Fine Arts Museum in Minsk, the State Museum of Fine Arts in Riga and the Fine Arts Museum in Odessa; in 1975-6 at the Fine Arts Museum in Caracas, the Italian Art Museum in Lima, the Seibu Museum of Art in Tokyo, the Kyoto Municipal Museum, the Fukouka Prefectural Cultural Center Museum of Art, and the Aichi Prefectural Museum of Art in Nagoya.

Since its first public exhibition in Memphis in 1969 the Collection has also been shown in whole or in part in Washington, D.C., Kansas City, Columbus, New Orleans, Little Rock, Oklahoma City, San Francisco, San Diego, Los Angeles, and Nashville, that is, not only in the large metropolitan centers that might enhance the prestige of the Collection, but also in the smaller communities whose residents have only rarely the opportunity to see paintings and drawings by the masters represented in it.

The catalog has grown along with the Collection. There have been two English editions, as well as a Russian edition, and bilingual editions in Spanish-English, Japanese-English, and French-English.

The present catalog is based on the 1971 edition with the original entries prepared for the most part by the staff of the Los Angeles County Museum of Art: Ebria Feinblatt, the drawings; Charles Millard, the nineteenth- and early twentieth-century European paintings; Larry Curry, the American paintings; and I prepared the entries for the old master paintings. The notes on the Raphael and Durer drawings were written by Dr. Konrad Oberhuber, formerly of the Albertina Graphics Collection, Vienna, and now professor of history of art at Harvard University; those on the Géricault portrait by Professor Lorenz Eitner of Stanford University; and those on the Rembrandt drawing by Dr. Christopher White, director of the Paul Mellon Center for Study of British Art, London. Edward Cornachio took the color transparencies. Jeanne D'Andrea and Joanne Jaffe followed the editing, designing, and production from manuscript to final book.

Our debts of gratitude are many: to John Walker for his introductory essay; to Dr. Oberhuber, Dr. Eitner, Dr. White, and the curatorial staff of the Los Angeles County Museum of Art for their catalog entries; to Mrs. Elizabeth Andrews, who furnished much of the documentation; to Carolyn H. Wells, research assistant to John Walker, who painstakingly reviewed the entries in the earlier Hammer catalogs at the Library of Congress; to Victor Hammer for his ready cooperation; to Sheri Hirst, who supervised the printing and design of the bilingual editions, to Martha Wade Kaufman, former curator of The Armand Hammer Collection and director of art of The Armand Hammer Foundation, currently art consultant to the Foundation, who has made numerous additions to the notes and bibliographies in the catalog revisions subsequent to 1971; and to Olga Hammer, present curator of The Armand Hammer Collection and director of art of The Armand Hammer Foundation, who is charged with the responsibility of the Collection in every aspect.

Speaking for the museum directors of four continents who have had the privilege of exhibiting the Hammer Collection, I would like to express especial appreciation to Dr. and Mrs. Armand Hammer for giving such rich experiences and so much joy to the people we serve.

Kenneth Donahue

Director, Los Angeles County Museum of Art

European Period

(Seventeenth - Twentieth Centuries)

Juno
Oil on canvas
50" x 48-3/4" (127.0 x 122.87 cm.)

REMBRANDT van Rijn (1606-1669)

Portrait of a Man of the Raman Family
Oil on oval panel
25-1/2" x 19-7/8" (64.8 x 50.5 cm.)

3   **Peter Paul RUBENS (1577-1640)**

Young Woman with Curly Hair
Oil on panel
28" x 20-1/2" (71.1 x 52.1 cm.)

The Israelites Gathering Manna in the Desert
Oil on panel
25-1/2" x 20-3/4" (64.8 x 52.7 cm.)

The Education of the Virgin
Oil on panel
11-13/16" x 9-5/8" (30.3 x 24.4 cm.)

El Pelele
Oil on canvas
14" x 9-1/8" (35.6 x 23.2 cm.)

Portrait of a Gentleman
Oil on canvas
25-5/8" x 21-1/4" (65.1 x 54.0 cm.)

8   Camille COROT (1796-1875)

Harvester Under Trees
Oil on canvas
15-13/16" x 12" (40.1 x 30.5 cm.)

Medieval Ruins
Oil on canvas, mounted on board
9" x 12" (23.0 x 30.5 cm.)

Distant View of Mantes Cathedral
Oil on canvas
22-1/16" x 18-1/16" (56.0 x 45.9 cm.)

Portrait of a Girl
Oil on canvas
12-1/4" x 9-3/16" (32.1 x 24.3 cm.)

12   Camille COROT (1796-1875)

Morning
Oil on canvas
69-11/16" x 52-3/8" (177.0 x 133.0 cm.)

Pleasures of Evening
Oil on canvas
44-1/2" x 65-3/16" (113.0 x 165.6 cm.)

14   Honoré DAUMIER (1808-1879)

The Lawyers (The Bar)
Oil on canvas
12-9/16" x 19-3/4" (32.5 x 50.0 cm.)

Beach at Trouville
Oil on canvas
12-7/8" x 7-5/16" (32.7 x 18.6 cm.)

Sailing Ships in Port
Oil on canvas
17-3/4" x 25-5/16" (45.1 x 64.3 cm.)

Salome
Oil on canvas
56-5/8" x 41-1/16" (143.8 x 104.2 cm.)

King David
Oil on canvas
90-9/16" x 54-5/16" (230.0 x 137.6 cm.)

20   Camille PISSARRO (1830-1903)

Boulevard Montmartre, Mardi Gras
Oil on canvas
25" x 31-1/2" (63.5 x 77.5 cm.)

21   Edgar DEGAS (1834-1917)

Three Dancers in Yellow Skirts
Oil on canvas
32" x 25-5/8" (81.3 x 65.1 cm.)

Peonies in a Blue and White Vase
Oil on canvas
23-15/16" x 19-5/8" (60.8 x 49.9 cm.)

Portrait of Miss Edith Crowe
Oil on canvas
28-3/4" x 23-5/16" (73.0 x 59.2 cm.)

Roses
Oil on canvas
26-1/16" x 22-11/16" (66.2 x 57.7 cm.)

Timber Yard at Saint-Mammès
Oil on canvas
21-1/2" x 28-3/4" (55.6 x 72.9 cm.)

Boy Resting
Oil on canvas
21-7/16" x 25-13/16" (54.5 x 65.5 cm.)

View of Bordighera
Oil on canvas
26" x 32-1/4" (66.0 x 81.9 cm.)

Portrait of "Paule Gobillard"
Niece of Berthe Morisot
Oil on canvas
28-3/4" x 23-3/4" (72.8 x 60.1 cm.)

Grape Pickers at Lunch
Oil on canvas
21-7/8" x 18-1/4" (55.5 x 46.4 cm.)

Antibes
Oil on canvas
25-1/2" x 32" (64.8 x 81.3 cm.)

Two Girls Reading
Oil on canvas
22" x 18-5/8" (55.9 x 47.2 cm.)

Square in Argenteuil
Oil on canvas
23-13/16" x 27-3/4" (60.5 x 70.5 cm.)

Bonjour M. Gauguin
Oil on canvas, mounted on panel
29-1/2" x 21-1/2" (74.9 x 54.6 cm.)

Garden of the Rectory at Nuenen
Oil on canvas, mounted on panel
20-7/8" x 30-3/4" (53.0 x 78.2 cm.)

Lilacs
Oil on canvas
10-3/4" x 13-15/16" (27.3 x 35.3 cm.)

The Sower
Oil on canvas
13-1/4" x 15-15/16" (33.6 x 40.4 cm.)

Hospital at Saint-Rémy
Oil on canvas
35-1/2" x 28" (90.2 x 71.1 cm.)

In the Salon
Oil on cardboard
15-3/4" x 23-7/8" (40.0 x 60.6 cm.)

Street Scene
Oil on canvas
21" x 27-1/2" (53.3 x 69.8 cm.)

Nude against the Light
Oil on canvas
48-3/4" x 21-1/2" (123.8 x 54.6 cm.)

41 Emile BERNARD (1868-1941)

Wheat Harvest
Oil on canvas
28-1/2" x 35-7/8" (72.4 x 91.1 cm.)

In the Bus
Oil on board
9-13/16" x 9" (25.0 x 22.9 cm.)

At the Seashore
Oil on panel
8-1/2" x 8-1/2" (21.6 x 21.6 cm.)

44   Edouard VUILLARD (1868-1940)

Rue Lepic, Paris
Tempera
65" x 18-1/2" (165.1 x 47.0 cm.)

Interior
Oil on board
21-1/8" x 15-7/8" (53.3 x 40.3 cm.)

Circus Girl
Oil on paper
25-3/4" x 20-11/16" (65.4 x 52.5 cm.)

Summer Bouquet
Oil on canvas
25-3/4" x 21-9/16" (65.4 x 54.7 cm.)

48   André DERAIN (1880-1954)

Still Life with Basket, Jug and Fruit
Oil on canvas
19-7/8" x 23-11/16" (50.5 x 60.1 cm.)

Woman of the People
Oil on canvas
39-1/4" x 25-3/8" (99.7 x 65.1 cm.)

Women in the Forest
Oil on canvas
31-7/8" x 39-5/8" (81.0 x 107.0 cm.)

Blue Angel
Gouache and pastel
20" x 26" (50.8 x 66.1 cm.)

The Valet
Oil on canvas
43-1/4" x 25" (110.3 x 63.5 cm.)

American Period

(Nineteenth - Twentieth Centuries)

Portrait of George Washington
Oil on canvas
44-1/8" x 34-1/2" (112.0 x 87.6 cm.)

54 William Michael HARNETT (1848-1892)

Still Life
Oil on panel
13-3/4" x 10-5/16" (34.9 x 26.2 cm.)

Portrait of Sebastiano Cardinal Martinelli
Oil on canvas, mounted on panel
78-5/16" x 59-15/16" (198.9 x 152.3 cm.)

Dr. Pozzi at Home
Oil on canvas
80-1/2" x 43-7/8" (204.5 x 111.5 cm.)

Portrait of Mrs. Edward L. Davis and Her Son, Livingston Davis
Oil on canvas
86" x 48" (218.4 x 121.9 cm.)

Summertime
Oil on canvas
28-7/8" x 39-3/8" (73.4 x 100.0 cm.)

On the Beach
Oil on canvas
26-3/4" x 39" (67.9 x 99.0 cm.)

60   Andrew WYETH (1917-   )

Brandywine Valley
Watercolor
21" x 29" (53.3 x 73.7 cm.)

Drawings, Pastels and Watercolors

(Sixteenth - Twentieth Centuries)

Tuft of Cowslips
Gouache on vellum
7-9/16" x 6-5/8" (19.2 x 16.8 cm.)

Sheet of Studies
Pen and brown ink over traces of black chalk
6-1/2" x 5-1/2" (16.4 x 13.8 cm.)

Male Nude (recto)
Black chalk
9-1/4" x 4" (23.3 x 10.0 cm.)

Male Nude (verso)
Black chalk

Study for a Fresco with Hosea and Jonah
Pen and brown wash, heightened with white
10-5/8" x 7-13/16" (26.2 x 19.8 cm.)

Female Head
Black chalk
12-7/8" x 8-7/8" (32.7 x 22.5 cm.)

Pendentive Study with Sts. Matthew and Jerome (recto)
Ink and red chalk
8-1/4" x 5-1/2" (21.0 x 14.0 cm.)

Study for the "Madonna della Scodella" (verso)
Ink and red chalk
7-15/16" x 5" (20.2 x 12.7 cm.)

A Biblical Subject
Pen and ink, brown wash, heightened with white
6-13/16" x 6-3/4" (17.3 x 17.2 cm.)

Studies of a Beggar Man and Woman
Pen and brown ink
5" x 4-3/8" (12.7 x 11.1 cm.)

Young Girl
Red and black chalk
8-1/2" x 5-3/4" (21.6 x 14.6 cm.)

Couple Seated on a Bank
Red, black, and white chalk on buff paper
9-1/2" x 13-3/4" (24.1 x 34.9 cm.)

St. Jerome in the Desert Listening to the Angels
Pen and brown ink, brown wash, heightened
with white, over black chalk on buff paper
16-3/4" x 10-7/8" (42.5 x 27.6 cm.)

Virgin and Child Adored by Bishops, Monks, and Women
Pen and bister wash over black chalk on white paper
16-3/4" x 11-13/16" (42.5 x 30.0 cm.)

Landscape with a Rustic Bridge
Black chalk heightened with white on buff paper
8" x 10-3/4" (20.3 x 27.3 cm.)

Venus Reclining against a Dolphin
Black chalk heightened with white
9" x 13-1/2" (22.8 x 34.3 cm.)

A Tired Mother with Two Children
Pen and brown ink over black lead
9" x 11" (22.5 x 27.8 cm.)

76   Jean-Honoré FRAGONARD (1732-1806)

Study for the Education of the Virgin
Charcoal
10-15/16 x 8-9/16" (sight) (27.8 x 21.7 cm.)

The Reading
Brown wash
11" x 8-1/4" (27.9 x 21.0 cm.)

Grandfather's Reprimand
Gray-brown wash over black chalk
13-1/2" x 17-3/4" (34.3 x 45.1 cm.)

The Little Preacher
Brown wash over black chalk
13-3/4" x 18-1/4" (34.9 x 46.7 cm.)

Visit to the Nurse
Chinese ink wash, heightened with watercolor
12" x 15" (30.5 x 38.1 cm.)

Mrs. Badham
Pencil on white wove paper
10-1/4" x 8-1/4" (26.0 x 21.0 cm.)

Third Class Carriage
Red chalk on blue paper
10-9/16" x 13" (26.7 x 33.0 cm.)

The Pleading Lawyer
Watercolor, ink, and gouache
6-1/4" x 8-1/2" (15.9 x 21.6 cm.)

Two Women and a Child
Pen and brown and black wash,
heightened with white chalk
8-1/4" x 7-1/16" (21.0 x 18.0 cm.)

Peasants Resting
Pastel
16-3/4" x 20-1/4" (42.5 x 51.4 cm.)

Beach Scene
Pencil and watercolor
4-5/8" x 9-7/16" (11.7 x 24.0 cm.)

Pea Harvest
Watercolor and charcoal
9" x 11" (22.8 x 27.9 cm.)

88   Camille PISSARRO (1830-1903)

Montmorency Road
Pencil
9-1/4" x 12-3/8" (23.5 x 31.4 cm.)

Man Wearing a Cloak (recto)
Charcoal
16" x 8-3/4" (40.6 x 19.7 cm.)

Man Wearing a Cloak (verso)
Charcoal
16" x 8-3/4" (40.6 x 19.7 cm.)

Jacquet
Pastel
10-1/4" x 8-1/4" (26.0 x 20.6 cm.)

Theater Box
Pastel
22" x 16-1/2" (56.0 x 41.0 cm.)

Laundresses Carrying Linen
Charcoal
17" x 23" (43.2 x 58.4 cm.)

93   Edgar DEGAS (1834-1917)

Laundress Carrying Linen
Pastel
24" x 36-1/2" (61.0 x 92.7 cm.)

Study of the "Ecorché" (recto)
Pencil
6-1/4" x 7" (15.9 x 17.8 cm.)

Page of Studies: The Father of the Artist (verso)
Pencil
10-3/4" x 7" (27.3 x 17.8 cm.)

Mont Ste. Victoire
Watercolor
6-7/16" x 10-5/8" (16.4 x 27.0 cm.)

Vase of Flowers
Pastel
15-3/4" x 12-3/8" (40.0 x 31.4 cm.)

Landscape at Pont-Aven
Brush and ink
12-1/2" x 17-1/4" (31.8 x 43.8 cm.)

Parau No Te Varau Ino (left)
Tahitian Legend (right)
Pen, brush, and India ink; two drawings on one sheet, side by side
6" x 3-1/2" (15.2 x 8.9 cm.)

Tahitian Heads
Pencil
6-3/8" x 4" (16.2 x 10.2 cm.)

100-A   *Breton Peasant*
       Pencil and crayon

On succeeding pages are sixteen sketches by Paul Gauguin (1848-1903) from a sketchbook he purchased in Rouen in 1884, and used intermittently in Denmark and Brittany between 1884 and 1888. The sketchbook contains 122 pages (6½″ x 4¼″; 16.5 x 10.8 cm.) including inside covers. Two of the pages are blank, three contain miscellaneous notes, one notes on color, eleven Gauguin's "Notes Synthétiques"—his first written statement on art theory. The remaining 105 pages are filled with 268 sketches of landscapes, houses, animals, and people, mostly from Brittany. Many of the images are used in pictures of the same period.

100-B   *Little Breton Boy*
Pencil and crayon

100-C   *Little Breton Boy*
Pencil and crayon

100-D   *Bridge at Pont-Aven (?)*
Pencil and crayon

100-E   *Two Breton Women*
Pencil and crayon

100-F   *Head and Hand of a Monkey*
Pencil and crayon

100-G   *Little Breton Boy with Goose*
Pencil and crayon

100-H *Little Breton Boy with Pail*
Pencil and crayon

100-I *Little Breton Boy with Pail*
Pencil and crayon

100-J   *Sketches of a Child*
   Ink

100-K   *Landscape*
   Ink

100-L   *Head of a Child and Self-Portrait*
Ink

100-M   *Head of a Child and Head of a Man*
(probably self-portrait)
Ink

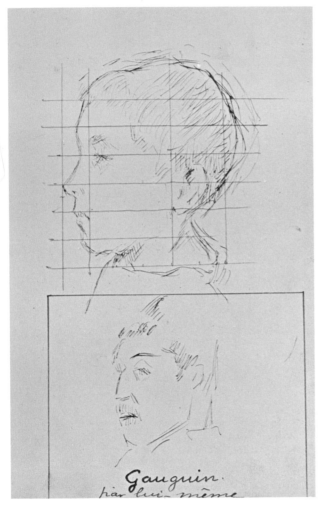

100-N   *Profile of Woman and Profile of Boy*
Ink

100-O   *Head of Woman, Tree, and Head of Man*
Ink

100-P   *Self-Portrait*
    Ink

Girlhood
Pencil
13-3/8" x 11-3/8" (34.0 x 28.9 cm.)

The Zandmennik House
Charcoal
9" x 11-3/4" (22.9 x 29.8 cm.)

The Magrot House, Cuesmes
Charcoal
9" x 11-3/4" (22.9 x 29.8 cm.)

Old Man Carrying a Bucket
Pencil heightened with gray and black wash
18-3/4" x 8-1/4" (47.6 x 21.0 cm.)

Man Polishing a Boot
Black chalk, pencil, heightened with white and gray wash
19" x 10-1/2" (48.3 x 26.7 cm.)

106 Henri-Edmond CROSS (1856-1910)

Cypresses
Gouache
9-1/2" x 13-1/4" (24.1 x 33.7 cm.)

Study after 'The Models'
Pen and ink
10-1/16" x 6-3/8" (26.0 x 16.5 cm.)

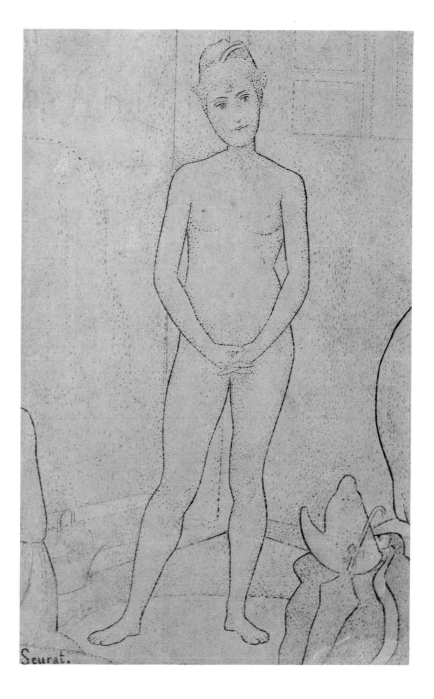

Girl Drying Her Knees
Pencil
13" x 9-1/2" (33.0 x 24.1 cm.)

109   Pablo PICASSO (1881-1973)

Female Nude (recto)
Pencil
6-1/2" x 4" (16.5 x 10.2 cm.)

Young Man (verso)
Pen and ink

Catalog of the Collection

CATALOG REFERENCE PAGE

The catalog of The Armand Hammer Collection has been printed for each exhibition and is registered with the Library of Congress in Washington, D. C. To avoid repetition the names of the museums, institutions and galleries where the Collection has been exhibited in its entirety are listed below and will be identified by Roman Numerals. (See each listing. All exhibitions are noted when not exhibited with the Collection. Exceptions are noted.) The Collection is housed at the Los Angeles County Museum of Art when it is not traveling and is frequently hung with the museum's permanent collection. These individual exhibition dates are not included as this information is readily available at the Los Angeles County Museum of Art.

I. NEW YORK CITY, New York, Hammer Galleries, 40th Anniversary Loan Exhibition, 1928-1968, November 7—December 7, 1968

II. MEMPHIS, Tennessee, Brooks Memorial Art Gallery, October 2—December 30, 1969

III. WASHINGTON, D.C., Smithsonian Institution, The Armand Hammer Collection, March 20—May 17, 1970

IV. KANSAS CITY, Missouri, William Rockhill Nelson Gallery of Art, June 30—August 2, 1970

V. NEW ORLEANS, Louisiana, Issac Delgado Museum of Art, August 15— September 20, 1970

VI. COLUMBUS, Ohio, Columbus Gallery of Fine Arts, October 9—November 1, 1970

VII. LITTLE ROCK, Arkansas, Arkansas Art Center, November 21, 1970—January 12, 1971

VIII. SAN FRANCISCO, California, California Palace of the Legion of Honor, February 11—March 14, 1971

IX. OKLAHOMA CITY, Oklahoma, Oklahoma Art Center, June 15—July 11, 1971

X. SAN DIEGO, California, Fine Arts Gallery of San Diego, July 23—September 5, 1971

XI. LOS ANGELES, California, Los Angeles County Museum of Art, December 21, 1971—February 27, 1972

XII. LONDON, England, Royal Academy of Arts, June 24—July 24, 1972

XIII. DUBLIN, Ireland, The National Gallery of Ireland, August 9—October 1, 1972

XIV. LENINGRAD, U.S.S.R., The Hermitage Museum, October 23—December 2, 1972

XV. MOSCOW, U.S.S.R., The Pushkin Museum, December 8, 1972—February 11, 1973

XVI. KIEV, U.S.S.R., State of Museum of Fine Art of the Ukraine Soviet Socialist Republic, March 6—March 31, 1973

XVII. MINSK, U.S.S.R., State Fine Art Museum, April 27—May 26, 1973

XVIII. RIGA, U.S.S.R., State Museum of Foreign Fine Arts, June 8—July 8, 1973

XIX. ODESSA, U.S.S.R., Fine Arts Museum, July 25—August 25, 1973

XX. LOS ANGELES, California, Los Angeles County Museum of Art, on exhibition, 19th and 20th Century Galleries, June 22—December 9, 1974

XXI. CARACAS, Venezuela, Fine Arts Museum, January 9—February 2, 1975

XXII. LIMA, Peru, Italian Art Museum, February 15—March 9, 1975

XXIII. LOS ANGELES, California, Los Angeles County Museum of Art, 10th Anniversary Show, April 9—June 29, 1975

XXIV. TOKYO, Japan, Ikebukuro-Seibu Museum, September 20—November 3, 1975

XXV. KYOTO, Japan, Municipal Museum of Art, November 10—December 20, 1975

XXVI. FUKOUKA, Japan, Fukouka Prefectural Culture Center Museum, January 4—February 1, 1976

XXVII. NAGOYA, Japan, Aichi Prefectural Museum, February 11—March 20, 1976

XXVIII. NASHVILLE, Tennessee, Tennessee Fine Arts Center at Cheekwood, June 12—August 15, 1976

XXIX. NASHVILLE, Tennessee, Cheekwood Extension, August 15—September 12, 1976

XXX. MEXICO CITY, Mexico, Palace of Fine Arts, February 21—March 15, 1977

XXXI. PARIS, France, Jacquemart-André Museum, March 29—July 25, 1977

XXXII. PARIS, France, Louvre Museum - Cabinet of Drawings, March 29—May 25, 1977

XXXIII. PARIS, France, Louvre Museum - Cabinet of Drawings and Jacquemart-André Museum, March 29—July 25, 1977

XXXIV. MALIBU, California, The J. Paul Getty Museum, September 13— October 29, 1977

XXXV. ATLANTA, Georgia, The High Museum of Art, November 20, 1977—January 22, 1978

XXXVI. COLORADO, Denver, The Denver Art Museum, February 18—April 9, 1978

1 REMBRANDT van Rijn (1606-1669)

Juno
Oil on canvas: 50″ x 48 3/4″ (127.0 x 122.87 cm.)

Collections: Harmen Becker, Amsterdam, ca. 1665-1678; J. Thos. Stanley of Palmerston House, Turnbridge near Sheffield, England (probably Sir John Thomas Stanley, First Baron Stanley of Alderly), 1735-1856; Otto Friedrich Ludwig Wesendonck, Berlin, before 1888-1896; Mathilde Wesendonck (his widow), Berlin, 1896-1903; Wesendonck heirs, 1903-1925; Provincial Museum, Bonn, 1925-1935; W. Poech and A. J. Schrender, Amsterdam, 1935; D. Katz, Dieren, Holland, 1935; C. J. K. van Aalst, K. B. E., Huis te Hoevelaken, Holland; N. J. van Aalst, Huis te Hoevelaken, Holland, 1966; Hans M. Cramer, The Hague, 1966; Mr. and Mrs. J. William Middendorf II, 1966-1976; The Armand Hammer Foundation, acq. 1976

Exhibited: Bonn, Provincial Museum, 1906-1935 (lent by Mr. and Mrs. Otto Wesendonck and heirs); Amsterdam, Rijksmuseum, *Internal Art Trade Exhibition,* 1935; New York Schaeffer Galleries, Inc., *Rembrandt,* April 1-15, 1937, no. 5 (repr. in cat.), (lent by D. Katz); New York, *World's Fair Masterpieces of European Paintings and Sculpture from 1300-1800,* May-Oct. 1939, no. 312 (p. 52 in cat. by G. H. McCall and W. R. Valentiner), (lent by C. J. K. van Aalst); Detroit Institute of Arts, *Masterpieces of Art from Foreign Collections,* (European Paintings from the New York and San Francisco World's Fairs), Nov. 10-Dec. 10, 1939, no. 40 (repr. in cat.), (lent by C. J. K. van Aalst). Circulated in 1940-41 to the Cleveland Museum of Art, Los Angeles County Museum of Art, Minneapolis Institute of Arts, Newark Museum, Springfield (Mass.) Museum, St. Louis City Art Museum; Detroit Institute of Arts, *Masterpieces of Art from European and American Collections* (European paintings from the New York and San Francisco World's Fairs), April 1-May 31, 1941, no. 49 (repr. p. 18 in cat.), (lent by C. J. K. van Aalst); Detroit Institute of Arts, 1941-1947, (lent by C. J. K. van Aalst); Los Angeles County Museum, *Frans Hals-Rembrandt,* Nov. 18-Dec. 31, 1947, no. 30 (p. 74 and 75 repr. pl. XXX, in cat. by W. R. Valentiner), (lent by estate of C. J. K. van Aalst); Rotterdam, Museum Boymans-van Beuningen, Mar.-May 1966 (lent by Mr. and Mrs. J. W. Middendorf II); New York, Metropolitan Museum of Art, mid-1966-1976, (lent by Mr. and Mrs. J. W. Middendorf II); New York, Wildenstein, *Gods & Heros, Baroque Images of Antiquity,* Oct. 30, 1968-Jan. 4, 1969, no. 34 (repr. in cat. in color frontispiece), (lent by Mr. and Mrs. J. W. Middendorf II); Tokyo, National Museum of Western Art, *The Age of Rembrandt, Dutch Paintings and Drawings of the 17th Century,* Oct. 19-Dec. 22, 1968, no. 52 (in cat.), (lent by Mr. and Mrs. J. W. Middendorf II); Kyoto, Municipal Museum, Jan. 12-Mar. 2, 1969, as above

Exhibitions: See catalog ref. page
First exhibited: XXX
Exhibited: Cambridge, Mass., Fogg Museum, Harvard University, Oct. 1-Dec. 1976; Los Angeles, Los Angeles County Museum of Art, New Acquisitions Gallery, Dec. 19-Feb. 6, 1977

Literature: N. De Roever, "Rembrandt, Bijdrogen tot de Geschiedenis van Zijn laatste levensjaren," *Oud Holland,* vol. II, 1884, pp. 90-91; O. Wesendonck, *Katalog A.* Gemalde Sammlung Wesendonck, Berlin, 1888, pp. 77-78, no. 240; A. Bredius, "Nievwe Rembrandtiana," *Oud Holland,* vol. XVII, 1899, p. 4; C. Hofstede de Groot, *Die Urkunden über Rembrandt,* (1575-1721), The Hague, 1906, pp. 337-338, no. 278, and *passim;* W. Cohen, "Die Sammlung Wesendonck," *Zeitschrift für Bildende Kunst,* NF vol. XXI, 1909, pp. 57 ff; A. Bredius " Rembrandtiana II: De Nalatenscap van Harmen Becker," *Oud Holland,* vol. XXVIII, 1910, pp. 195 ff; W. Cohen, *Katalog der Gemäldegalerie vorwiegend Sammlung Wesendonck,* Bonn, Provinzial-museum, 1914, p. 156, no. 230; C. Hofstede de Groot, *A Catalog Raisonné of the Works of the Most Eminent Dutch Painters of the Seventeenth Century,* vol. VI, London, 1916, p. 138, no. 207a; W. Cohen, *Katalog der Gemäldegalarie vorwiegend Sammlung Wesendonck,* Bonn, Provinzial-museum, 2nd ed. 1927, p. 154, no. 230; Sale catalog, *Westdeutscher Museumbesitz, Sammlung Wesendonck von Bissing,* Cologne, Math. Lempertz, Nov. 27, 1935, p. 26, no. 87 repr.; A. Bredius, "Ein wildergefundener Rembrandt," *Pantheon,* vol. XVIII, 1936, p. 277, repr.; A. Bredius, *The Paintings of Rembrandt,* London, 1936, p. 27, no. 639, repr.; G. Isarlo, "La Junon de Rembrandt est retrouvée," *Beaux-Arts,* Oct. 9, 1936, p. 2, repr.; A. Heppner, "Ein Rembrandt Entdeckung," *Die Weltkunst,* vol. 8, no. 31-32, Aug. 9, 1936, p. 1, repr.; J. L. A. A. M. dan Ryckevorsel "De Teruggevonden Schilderij van Rembrandt: De Juno," *Oud Holland,* vol. LIII, 1936, pp. 270-274, repr. pl. l.; H. G. Fell, "The 'Juno' of Rembrandt" Editorial *Connoisseur,* vol. XCIX, Jan.-June 1937, p. 3, repr. in color cover and frontispiece (includes letters by A. Bredius and W. R. Valentiner); A. M. Frankfurter, "An Important View of Rembrandt," *The Art News,* vol. XXXV, no. 27, April 3, 1937, pp. 9, 24, 25, repr. p. 8; Anon. "Rembrandt's 'Juno'," *The Art Designer,* vol. XI, no. 13, April 1, 1937, p. 12 repr.; J. Held, "Two Rembrandts," *Parnassus,* vol. IX, no. 4, April 1937, pp. 36-38, repr.; M. Weinberger, " 'New' Rembrandts" *Magazine of Art,* vol. XXX, 1937, p. 312-314, repr. p. 299; John Rewald, " A l'étranger un Rembrant vendu par un musée allemand." *Amour de l'art,* vol. XIX, no. 9, Nov. 1938, p. 361, repr.; W. R. Valentiner & A. M. Frankfurter, *Masterpieces of Art Exhibition at the New York World's Fair 1939* —Guide and Picture Book, New York, 1939, repr. p. 96; E. Kieser, "uber Rembrandts Verhältnis zur Antiko," *Zeitschrift für Kunstgeschichte,* vol. X, 1941/2, p. 141; J. Rosenberg, *Rembrandt,* Cambridge, Mass., 1948, vol. l, p. 248, concordance; G. Knuttel, *Rembrandt, De meester en zijn werk,* Amsterdam, 1956, pp. 210, 278; Anon., "Rembrandt's 'Lost' Juno to be Auctioned at Christie's," *Arts,* vol. XXXIV, no. 5, Feb. 1960, p. 9; N. Maclaren, *The Dutch School*, National Gallery Catalog, London, 1960, p. 313; Anon., "Rembrandt's 'Juno' für das Metropolitan Museum," *Die Weltkunst*, vol. XXXVI, no. 7, April 1, 1966, p. 291 repr.; Sale catalog, *Highly Important Netherlandish Paintings from the Collection Formed by the late Dr. C. J. K. van Aalst*, London, Christie's, April 1, 1960, pp. 26-27, no. 38, repr. pl. 18 and color frontispiece (bought in); G. Cramer Galerie, *Catalogue No. XII 1965-66*, The Hague, 1965, p. 7, repr.; G. C. V. "Rembrandt 'Juno' in den Haag," *Die Weltkunst*, vol. XXXV, no. 21, Nov. 15, 1965, pp. 1091-2; K. Bauch, *Rembrandt Gemälde*, Berlin, 1966, pp. xv, 15, no. 285, repr. pl. 285; Ann Livermore, "Rembrandt and Jansen: A New Interpretation," *Apollo*, vol. LXXXV, Jan.-June 1967, p. 245, n. 4; H. Gerson, *Rembrandt's Paintings*, New York, 1968, p. 132, 133, repr. in color, 430 no. 374, 431, repr.; S. Nodelman, "After the High Roman Fashion," *Art News*, vol. LXVII, no. 7, Nov. 1968, pp. 34 ff., repr.; M. S. Young, "Letter from U.S.A.," *Apollo*, vol. LXXXVII, Jul.-Dec. 1968, p. 390; J. J. Jacobs, "New York Gallery Notes," *Art in America*, vol. LVI, no. 6, Nov.-Dec. 1968, p. 109, repr. in color; J. T. Butler, "The American Way with Art," *The Connoisseur*, vol. CLXIX, no. 681, Nov. 1968, p. 200, repr.; A. Bredius, revised by H. Gerson, *Rembrandt, The Complete Edition of the Paintings*, London, 1969, p. 617, no. 639, repr. p. 396; J. Held, *Rembrandt's Aristotle and Other Rembrandt Studies*, Princeton, 1969, chap. III "Juno", pp. 85-103, repr.; B. Haak, *Rembrandt, His Life, His Work, His Time*, New York, 1969, p. 318, repr. in color p. 318, pl. 539; E. Haverkamp-Begemann, "The Present State of Rembrandt Studies," *Art Bulletin*, vol. LIII, (1971), p. 95

Juno, considered one of the finest works of Rembrandt's late period according to Seymour Slive, appears as a regal figure wearing a golden crown and sumptuously jeweled in a golden brown brocade gown. Over her shoulders is draped a fur lined robe. She is a very womanly figure of ample proportions and depicted with a wise, reflective yet benevolent expression. Her right hand rests on a scepter, the lower end of which directs attention to the half hidden peacock, Juno's sacred bird —symbol of wealth. Only with the presence of the symbolic bird is her identity as Juno confirmed. Her dress is theatrical in its opulence and its generalized design is typical of Rembrandt's costume stylization, enriched by textural qualities ranging from full impasto to subtle glazing, as described by Mr. Slive.

Rembrandt makes no effort to utilize classical forms or to recreate an ancient portrait. Nor does he flaunt the goddess' allegorical or historical role or her attributes. The sitter's identity remains unknown, but her presence is unforgettable. It is said she bears a resemblance to Hendrickje Stoffels, Rembrandt's common-law wife. Had Rembrandt taken Miss Stoffels as his second wife, he would have lost his inheritance from his first wife's (Saskia) estate according to Julius Held.

The prototype behind Rembrandt's allegorical portrait comes not from antiquity but from the Seventeenth Century E. Haverkamp-Begeman has observed that Rembrandt based the sitter's pose, with the right hand resting on a scepter and the left arched outward from her body, on an etching by Wenzel Hollar which reproduced Elsheimer's painting entitled, "The Realm of Juno." (See Rembrandt's so-called "Portrait of Anna Wymer as Minerva," *Studies in Western Art*, 1963, III, 63, fn. 12.)

Agnes Mongan has noted a resemblance between the model for *Juno* and the so-called "Catherine Cornaro" by Titian (Cook Collection, Richmond). Although Kenneth Clark does not discuss this possible instance of Titianesque influence, he does mention that Rembrandt owned a "very large book" of engravings after Titian's paintings. (See *Rembrandt and the Italian Renaissance*, London, 1966.)

Rembrandt painted this *Juno* for the art collector Harmen Becker, who complained in the spring of 1665 to the artist that the painting was still unfinished. Mr. Slive attributes this criticism to the fact that the mature painter's conception of a finished painting was a world apart from the one held by most of his contemporaries. In Rembrandt's opinion, a painting was finished when the artist had completed his intentions, said Mr. Slive. It was in Becker's estate in 1678 when the inventory of his goods was taken.

"The picture" says Mr. Slive, "is one of the few directly traceable to Rembrandt's studio." *Juno* disappeared for more than 200 years after the death of its original owner, Harmen Becker, in 1678. It was sold for $214 by the Bonn Museum at a Cologne auction in 1935 when it was incorrectly cataloged as "style of Rembrandt" because its qualities were hidden by repaint and discolored varnish.

In fact, there were two Junos in his collection: A "Juno, life size" (no name of painter) and a "Juno by Rembrandt van Rijn." The painting was lost after that, but it came to light again at the Wesendonck sale, Cologne, November 27, 1935, lot 87 ("in the manner of Rembrandt") after having been (but not on exhibition) in the Museum in Bonn. Recent cleaning shows it to be as great in beauty as Lucretia pictures of the same period. Held, in his exhaustive study of paintings, supposes that the picture was begun before 1660 and finished around 1665.

2 REMBRANDT van Rijn (1606-1669)

Portrait of a Man of the Raman Family, 1634
Oil on oval panel: 25 1/2" x 19 7/8" (64.8 x 50.5 cm.), enlarged to rectangle 27 1/8" x 21" (68.9 x 53.3 cm.)
Signed and dated lower right: Rembrandt fe 1634
Inscribed lower left: Aet. 47

Collections: The Raman family, Amsterdam; August de Ridder, Schönberg near Cronberg; Kleinberger Galleries, Paris; Enrich Galleries, New York; Swiss private collector; Julius Weitzner Galleries, New York; P. de Boer, Amsterdam; H. Kohn, Wassenaar, Holland; H. Shickman Gallery, New York; Los Angeles County Museum of Art (Frances and Armand Hammer Purchase Fund, 1969)

Exhibited: Frankfurt am Main, Städelsches Kunstinstitut, 1911-1913 (following death of de Ridder, May 13, 1911); New York, F. Kleinberger Galleries, *The Collection of Pictures of the Late Herr A. de Ridder,* exhibition and private sale Nov. 24-Dec. 15, 1913, No. 1 (repr. in cat. p. 32); Detroit Institute of Arts, *Paintings by Rembrandt,* May 2-31, 1930, no. 22 (repr. in cat.), (lent by the Ehrich Galleries, New York); The Hague, Mauritshuis, Mar.-Apr., 1946, no. 46; Basel, Katz Galerie, *Rembrandt Austellung,* July 24-Sept. 30, 1948, no. 13 (repr. in cat.), (lent by Swiss private collector); Raleigh, North Carolina Museum of Art, Nov. 16-Dec. 30, 1956, no. 9 (repr. in cat.), (lent by Julius Weitzner, New York)

Exhibitions: See catalog ref. page
First Exhibited: II
Not Exhibited: IV, V, VI, VII, VIII, IX, X, XX

Literature: W. R. Valentiner, *Rembrandt, des Meisters Gemälde,* 3rd edition, (Klassiker der Kunst), Stuttgart/Berlin: 1909, repr. p. 193 as "Portrait of a Man"; Wilhelm Bode, *Die Gemäldegalerie des Herrn A. de Ridder,* Berlin: Julius Bard, 1910, p. 4, 35, repr. pl. 1 as "Portrait of a Man of the Raman Family"; Wilhelm Bode, *The Collection of Pictures of the Late Herr A. de Ridder* (trans. Harry Virgin), Berlin: Julius Bard, 1913, no. 1, repr. pl. 1; Hofstede de Groot, *A Catalogue Raisonné of the Works of the Most Eminent Dutch Painters of the Seventeenth Century,* London: Macmillan, 1916 vol. VI, p. 347, no. 739 as "A Man in a Large Slouch Hat, said to be a member of the Raman family"; Sale catalog, *Catalogue des tableaux anciens . . . composant la Galerie de feu M. A. de Ridder,* Paris: Galerie Georges Petit, June 2, 1924, no. 55, repr.; A. Bredius, *Rembrandt Gemälde,* Vienna: Phaidon, 1935, no. 194; A. Bredius, *The Paintings of Rembrandt,* Vienna: Phaidon, 1937, no. 194: Jakob Rosenberg, *Rembrandt,* Cambridge: Harvard University Press, 1948, vol. I, p. 243 (concordance); Kurt Bauch, *Rembrandt Gemälde,* Berlin, 1966, de Gruyter, p. 19 (notes), no. 374, repr. no. 374; Horst Gerson, *Rembrandt Paintings,* Amsterdam and New York: Reynal & Co., 1968, p. 495, no. 168, repr. p. 289; Horst Gerson (ed.), *Rembrandt, The Complete Edition of the Paintings of Rembrandt by A. Bredius,* London: Phaidon, 1969, p. 564, no. 194, repr. p. 158

———————————

The sitter has been called a member of the Raman family since, according to Bode, 1910, the painting came directly from the old Amsterdam patrician family, Raman, to the de Ridder collection. It had presumably been in that family from the time it was painted. The picture does not

appear in the Rembrandt literature until Valentiner included it in the third edition of the Klassiker der Kunst *Rembrandt* in 1909. By that time it had already been enlarged from its original shape to a rectangle. In subsequent literature (Hofstede de Groot, 1916; Bauch, 1966; Gerson, 1968; Gerson-Bredius, 1969) the statement is made that the painting was originally ten-sided. If that were true, the enlargement would follow a simple decagonal pattern. X-rays show, however, a quite irregular twelve-sided pattern which suggests that the painting was originally an oval, approximately the same as that shown in the present frame. Cleaning has also shown the present original to be oval rather than decagonal. This is clearly visible in the reproduction of Bredius, 1937.

Bode, 1910, noted the extraordinary fine state of preservation of the picture. This has been attested in a recent cleaning at the Los Angeles County Museum of Art. *The Portrait of a Lady in a Broad Ruff,* 1636, reported as in the collection of Kinnaird, Rossie Priory (Bredius no. 354) has been considered in the Rembrandt literature from Hofstede de Groot on to be a companion to the Hammer portrait.

3 Peter Paul RUBENS (1577-1640)

Young Woman with Curly Hair, ca. 1618-1620
Oil on panel: 17 1/16" x 13 3/16"
(43.3 x 33.5 cm.), enlarged to 28" x 20 1/2" (71.1 x 52.1 cm.)

Collections: Schamp d'Aveschoot, Ghent (recorded 1830); Duc d'Arenberg and descendants, Brussels and later South of France (purchased 1840 at Schamp sale); Edward Speelman, London (bought 1959 from present Duke); Jean Davray, Paris

Exhibitions: See catalog ref. page
First Exhibited: II
Not Exhibited: XX
Exhibited: Rotterdam, Boymans Museum, *Olieverfschelsen van Rubens,* Dec. 19, 1953-Feb. 14, 1954, no. 73 (cat. by E. Haverkamp Bergemann, pp. 85, 86, repr. pl. 63); Bordeaux, May 19-July 31, 1954, *Flandres, Espagne, Portugal du XVème au XVIIème Siècle,* 1954, no. 80 (p. 83 in cat.); Brussels, Musées Royaux des Beaux-Arts de Belgique, *Le Siècle de Rubens,* Oct. 15-Dec. 12, 1965, no. 225 (pp. 215, 216 in cat. by Leo can Puyvelde, repr.)

Literature: John Smith, *Catalogue Raisonné of the Works of the Most Eminent Dutch, Flemish and French Painters,* vol. II (Rubens); London: Smith & Son, 1830, pp. 260-261, no. 881; and vol. IX (Supplement), 1842, p. 330, no. 317; Sale catalog, *Catalogue des tableaux...composant la galerie de M. Schamp d'Aveschoot, de Gand,* Sept. 14, 1840, p. 2; Max Rooses, *L'oeuvre de P. P. Rubens,* Antwerp, 1886-1892, vol. IV, pp. 138; 290, no. 1088; J. Nève, "Quelques Portraits de la Galerie d'Arenberg," *Annales de l'Académie Royale d'Archeologie de*

Belgique, Antwerp: vol. V, 4th series, vol. X (1897), pp. 275, 276; Max Rooses, "Oeuvres de Rubens— Addenda," *Bulletin Rubens,* Antwerp: vol. 5 (1909), pp. 83-84; Rudolf Oldenbourg, *P. P. Rubens,* Munich, Berlin, 1922, p. 142; Ludwig Burchard, "Portrait of a Young Woman with Curly Hair by Peter Paul Rubens," manuscript report on Arenberg-Hammer painting, ca. 1960; Douglas Cooper (ed.), *Great Private Collections,* New York: Macmillan, 1963, repr. p. 257; Michael Jaffé, manuscript letter to Roland Balay, M. Knoedler & Co., New York, dated: Cambridge University, Feb. 3, 1967; Michael Harvard, "Portrait of a Girl with Curly Hair by Rubens," manuscript report on the Arenberg-Hammer and Morris paintings, London: March, 1969; Michael Jaffé, "The Girl with the Golden Hair," *Apollo,* vol. XC, no. 92, Oct. 1969, pp. 310-313, repr. in color p. 311

The portrait as Rubens painted it was only the head and shoulders of the young woman. A Seventeenth-Century copy in the museum in Cassel shows the portrait in its original size. Sometime in the seventeenth or early eighteenth century the bevelled edge, about one inch all around, was trimmed off and the painting was set into a larger panel a little towards the top and right of center. The new panel seems to have been an oval, to which wedges were then or later added to make the present rectangle.

The identity of the sitter is not known. Jaffé believes that the painting is a study rather than a formal portrait. According to Burchard, Rubens made a second study of the same girl but in a more frontal pose (Munich, Alte Pinakothek, no. 793 in cat.; exhibited in Bamberg Museum in 1934). The Munich painting measures 18 7/8″ x 14 1/2″, approximately the same as the Hammer painting originally and, in Burchard's opinion, was probably painted at the same sitting.

The Hammer picture must have been extraordinarily popular in the Seventeenth and Eighteenth Centuries, for at least six early repetitions of it are known: the Cassel copy of the original before enlargement (canvas 17 1/4″ x 13 3/4″, no. 89 in cat. of 1888); four repetitions of the present enlarged image: Dresden Museum (panel 25 1/4″ x 19 1/2″, no. 964A in cat. of 1908, repr. Adolf Rosenberg, *P.P. Rubens, des Meisters Gemälde* (Klassiker der Kunst), second edition, Stuttgart/Leipzig, 1906, p. 373); Leningrad, Hermitage (canvas said to have been transferred from panel 26″ x 21 1/4″, no. 577 in cat. of 1901, with additional drapery across chest and near shoulder); Althrop, The Earl Spencer Collection (with two jeweled clasps holding bodice); Kiel, Prof. Götz Martins (panel 22 7/8″ x 16 7/8″), similar to Spencer portrait; and a sixth painting still further enlarged in the collection of John C. Morris, Richmond, Surrey. The Morris painting (panel 28″ x 23 1/4″) (repr. in Rudolf Oldenbourg, *P.P. Rubens, des Meisters Gemälde* Klassiker der Kunst) fourth edition, Berlin/Leipzig, 1921, p. 201) has a slightly lower neckline and extends

the torso almost to the hips. Michael Jaffé believes that all these repetitions of the enlarged picture were made after Rubens' death and that only the Hammer picture is an original by Rubens.

4   Peter Paul RUBENS (1577-1640)

The Israelites Gathering Manna in the Desert, 1625-1628
Oil on panel: 25 1/2″ x 20 3/4″ (64.8 x 52.7 cm.)

Collections: Isabella Clara Eugenia, Archduchess of the Spanish Netherlands, Brussels; Philip IV and Charles II of Spain; Don Francisco Casimiro Pimentel, Conde de Benavente, who in 1700, following the death of Charles II, received this and the other paintings from the Royal Collections kept in the Pieza de las Furias for himself and his successors; Dukes of Pastrana, Madrid, by inheritance from the Counts of Benavente; Emile Pacully, Paris (acquired from Duc de Pastrana, Madrid, probably at sale of 1888); Baron Robert Gendebien, Brussels (acquired from A. Stein, dealer, Paris); Rosenberg & Stiebel, New York; Los Angeles County Museum of Art (Frances and Armand Hammer Purchase Fund, 1969)

Exhibited: Rotterdam, Boymans Museum,*Olieverfschelsen van Rubens,* Dec. 19, 1953-Feb. 14, 1954, no. 73 (cat. by E. Haverkamp Bergemann, pp. 85, 86, repr. pl. 63); Bordeaux, May 19-July 31, 1954, *Flandres, Espagne, Portugal du XVe au XVIIe Siècle,* 1954, no. 80 (p. 83 in cat.); Brussels, Musées Royaux des Beaux-Arts de Belgique, *Le Siècle de Rubens,* Oct. 15-Dec. 12, 1965, no. 225 (pp. 215, 216 in cat. by Leo van Puyvelde, repr.)

Exhibitions: See catalog ref. page
First Exhibited: II
Not Exhibited: IV, V, VI, VII, VIII, IX, X, XX

Literature: Max Rooses, *L'Oeuvre de Pierre-Paul Rubens,* Antwerp, 1886-1892, vol. I, p. 73; Max Rooses, "De Verzameling Pacully de Paris," *Onze Kunst,* 1903, pp. 121-122; Virgile Josz, "La Collection Emile Pacully," *Les Arts,* 2nd year, no. 16, Apr. 1903, p. 35, repr. p. 36; Sale catalog, *Collection Emile Pacully, tableaux anciens et modernes,* Paris: Galerie Georges Petit, May 4, 1903, pp. 62-63, repr. with added garland; N. Sentenac y Cantanas, *La pintura en Madrid desde sus origenes hasta el signo XIX,* Madrid, 1907, pp. 78 ff.: History and inventory of Pastrana collection; Sale catalog, *Tableaux... dépendant de la succession de Monsieur E. Pacully,* Paris: Hôtel Drouot, July 5, 1938, no. 28, repr. with added garland, as by Rubens and Jan Brueghel (This and several other pictures from the 1903 sale were apparently bought back by the owner and kept through his lifetime); Leo von Puyvelde, *Les Esquisses de Rubens,* Basel: Holbein, 1940, p. 31, no. 7 (Engl. trans. London, 1947, p. 29); Egbert Haverkamp Begemann, "Rubens Schetsen," *Bulletin Museum Boymans Rotterdam,* vol. V. no. 1, Mar. 1954, p. 9, repr. p. 11; Victor H. Elbern, "Die Rubensteppiche des Kölner Domes, ihre Geschichte und ihre Stellung im Zyklus

Triumph der Eucharistie," *Kölner Domblatt,* vol. X, 1955, pp. 74-75, repr. pl. 29

About 1625 the Archduchess Isabella Clara Eugenia, daughter of Philip II of Spain and ruler of the Spanish Netherlands, commissioned Rubens to produce eleven huge paintings and several smaller ones to be used as cartoons (full size patterns) for a series of tapestries glorifying the Eucharist which she wished to present to the Convent of the Descalzas Reales (Franciscan Clarissa Nuns) in Madrid. The subjects were: four Old Testament prefigurations of the New Testament Eucharist, one of which was the Israelites gathering manna in the desert; two of the Evangelists and Eucharistic teachers and defenders; and five Eucharistic triumphs. The first series of tapestries made in Brussels was sent to the Convent in Madrid in July 1628. A second series is now in the Cathedral of Cologne. Other individual panels were woven.

In the preparation of the cartoons Rubens first painted rough sketches in grisaille, then full-color sketches *(modelli)* which were enlarged by the master and his shop to the desired size of the tapestry. The first sketch for *The Israelites Gathering Manna in the Desert* is a panel 5 3/4″ x 4 7/8″ in the Musée Bonnat, Bayonne. In it Moses is in the background of a composition with a strong movement from left to right. In preparing the Los Angeles *modello* Rubens centralized the composition, confining it between Moses on the right and the woman with the child who turns towards center on the left. The woman is adapted from the woman with a jug in the Raphael *Fire in the Borgo* in the Vatican; other elements in both the grisaille and the *modello* are related to a Rubens drawing in the Louvre (Lugt no. 1038, fig. 52, also repr. Elbern, 1958, fig. 12) after a Giulio Romano *Gathering of the Manna.* Employing Renaissance elements and classic compositional limits, Rubens has filled his stage with a dynamic movement and counter-movement of form, light, and psychology not possible before the Seventeenth Century.

In 1648 Philip IV asked that the large cartoons and "other small paintings" for the Triumph of the Eucharist series be sent to Madrid. It is assumed by Rubens scholars that the sketches which were in the Royal Collections of Spain in the late seventeenth century, including the Los Angeles *modello,* were sent at that time. Presumably before 1648, the Los Angeles *modello* was set into a larger panel and surrounded by a garland of flowers and fruits. Max Rooses' *(Onze Kunst,* 1903) attribution of the garland, formerly called Jan Brueghel, to Pieter Gysels (1621-1690), would imply a date in the late forties. The *modello* with the garland is reproduced in the two Pacully sale catalogs and in *Les Arts,* 1903. The enlargement was removed and the painting restored to its original size after the sale of 1938.

The Los Angeles *modello* was separated from the other Triumph of the Eucharist *modelli* now in the Prado when it was inherited by the Conde de Benavente. The Los Angeles *modello* had presumably been sold to Pacully before the Duchess of Pastrana presented a number of Rubens sketches for the Torre de la Parada from the same Benavente-Pastrana inheritance to the Prado on May 28, 1889 (Prado nos. 2038-2040).

The large cartoon (canvas, 192″ x 163″) made from the Los Angeles *modello* was one of six cartoons sent in 1648 to Philip IV. He presented the six to Olivares, who placed them in his small family church at Loeches, near Madrid. They were removed by French troops during the Napoleonic invasions. Two became the property of the Louvre; four, including *The Israelites Gathering Manna in the Desert,* were sold in 1818 to the Duke of Westminster and in 1928 to John Ringling for the Ringling Museum in Sarasota, Florida (repr. William E. Suida, *A Catalogue of Paintings in the John and Mable Ringling Museum of Art,* Sarasota, 1949, pp. 178-183). A copy of the Los Angeles *modello* is in the Museum of Doornik (Tournai). A School of Rubens drawing of the composition is in the Louvre (Lugt no. 1127).

The most concise study of the series in English is Julius Held, "Rubens' Triumph of the Eucharist and the *Modello* in Louisville," *J.B. Speed Art Museum Bulletin,* vol. XXVI, no. 3 (Feb. 1968). The most exhaustive studies are Elias Tormo, *En las Descalzas Reales de Madrid,* Tomo II, Fasiculo II, "Los Tapices: La Apoteosis Eucaristica de Rubens," Madrid: Junta de Iconografia Nacional, 1945; and Victor H. Elbern, "Die Rubensteppiche des Kölner Domes, ihre Geschichte und ihre Stellug in Zyklus Triumph der Eucharistie," *Kölner Domblatt,* X, 1955, pp. 43-88; XIV/XV, 1958, p. 121 ff.; XXI/XXII, 1963, pp. 77 ff.

5 Jean-Honoré FRAGONARD (1732-1806)

The Education of the Virgin, 1748-1752
Oil on panel: 11 13/16″ x 9 5/8″ (30.3 x 24.4 cm.)

Collections: J.B.P. Lebrun, Paris; Fontaine, Paris; Charles T...., Paris; Camille Groult, Paris; Wildenstein & Co., Inc., New York; Mr. and Mrs. Henry R. Luce, New York

Exhibited: New Haven, Yale University Art Gallery, *Pictures Collected by Yale Alumni,* May 8-June 18, 1956, no. 19 (repr. in cat.)

Exhibitions: See catalog ref. page
First Exhibited: II
Not Exhibited: X, XX, XXIII

Literature: Sale catalog, *Catalogue d'objets rares et curieux, provenant du Cabinet et Fonds de Marchandises de M. Lebrun par cessation de Commerce,* Paris: Galerie de M. Lebrun,

Sept. 29, 1806, no. 150; Pierre de Nolhac, *J-H Fragonard,* Paris: Goupil & Cie, 1906, p. 164; Georges Wildenstein, *The Paintings of Fragonard,* Phaidon, 1960, p. 195, no. 18, repr. pl.1

Fragonard used this subject for at least three paintings: an unfinished picture in a private collection, 35 1/2″ x 28 3/8″ (Wildenstein, no. 17); another version in the California Palace of the Legion of Honor, San Francisco, 32 1/4″ x 45 5/8″ at present, but probably cut down between 1793 and 1806 (Wildenstein, no. 19); and the Hammer picture. They were all executed presumably between 1748 and 1752 when the young Fragonard was a pupil of Boucher. The Hammer picture, which has the freshness and freedom of execution of a sketch, seems to be the artist's first statement of the image. It may then have become the model for the larger unfinished picture which corresponds closely to it in composition. The San Francisco version, more academic in its drawing, modeling, and light, seems to be the final distillation of the idea.

The drawing "The Study for the Education of the Virgin," has recently been added to the collection and is number 66 in this catalog.

6   Francisco GOYA (1746-1828)

El Pelele, ca. 1791
Oil on canvas: 14″ x 9 1/8″ (35.6 x 23.2 cm.)

Collections: Doña Beatriz Sánchez de la Fuente de Lafora, Madrid; Don Juan de Lafora, Madrid; M. Knoedler & Co., New York; Mr. and Mrs. Henry R. Luce, New York

Exhibited: Madrid, Sociedad Española de Amigos del Arte, *Bocetos y Estudias para Pinturas y Esculturas,* May-June, 1949, no. 109, catalog by F. J. Sánchez-Canton; New Haven, Connecticut, Yale University Art Gallery, *Pictures Collected by Yale Alumni,* May 8-June 18, 1956, no. 29 (repr. in cat.)

Exhibitions: See catalog ref. page
First Exhibited: II
Not Exhibited: X, XX, XXII

Literature: August L. Mayer, *Francisco de Goya,* Munich: F. Bruckmann, 1923, p. 210, no. 570a, Engl. trans. London and Toronto: J.M. Dent, 1924, p. 176, no. 570a; Valentin de Sambricio, *Tápices de Goya,* Madrid: Patrimonio Nacional, Archivo General del Palacio, 1946, p. 273, no. 58a, repr. pl. CLXXXIV

In 1776 Goya began a series of oil paintings of Spanish popular life to be used as cartoons for forty-six tapestries by the Real Fábrica de Tápices de Santa
Bárbara in Madrid. The large cartoons are preserved in the Prado. *El Pelele* (Prado no. 802, 105″ x 63″), painted about 1791, was one of the last three cartoons delivered. The tapestry, today in the Palace of El Prado, was executed in 1793. There are two known *bocetos* for the Prado cartoon, one in the collection of Mrs. R. H. Kress (17 1/2″ x 10″), the other in this collection. The Hammer picture is presumably the first concept of the subject, with its freely sketched figures and the pentimenti in the straw man. Especially noticeable is the change in the position of the left foreleg. The group stands in an open space before a wall at the left and with the slightest indication of foliage at the right. In the Kress picture the figures are close to those in the Hammer picture; the primary difference is in the development of a more airy and spacious background. The wall has receded and a large shrub has grown between it and the figure group to indicate the extension of space. In the Prado cartoon the straw man has assumed a new and more limp position, the dresses and features of the four girls have been considerably elaborated, the wall has now become a palace in the far distance, and delicate shrubbery creates a broad and deep landscape so that the straw man can be more effectively silhouetted against the sky.

This may well have been one of the "Diez y seis bocetos pequeños de los tápices" listed in the inventory of the personal property of Francisco Goya in Madrid inherited by his son Javier Goya (Inventory published in X. Despartmet Fitz-Gerald, *L'Oeuvre peint de Goya,* Paris: F. de Nobele, 1928-50, text vol. I, pp. 53-54).

7   Théodore GERICAULT (1791-1824)

Portrait of a Gentleman
Oil on canvas: 25 5/8″ x 21 1/4″ (65.1 x 54.0 cm.)
Signed lower left: T.G.

Collections: Christie, Manson & Woods, London; Le Bohélec, Paris; Sale, Paris, Galerie Charpentier, June 16, 1955; Drs. Fritz and Peter Nathan, Zurich

Exhibited: Winterthur, Kunstmuseum, Theodore Géricault, 1953, no. 92; Los Angeles, Los Angeles County Museum of Art, Géricault, October 12-December 12, 1971, no. 3 (repr.)

Exhibitions: See catalog ref. page
First Exhibited: XI
Not Exhibited: XX
Exhibited: Detroit, Michigan, The Detroit Institute of Arts, Géricault Collection, Jan. 23-Mar. 7, 1972; Philadelphia, Pennsylvania, Philadelphia Museum of Art, Géricault Collection, Mar. 30-May 14, 1972

Literature: C. Clément, *Géricault, étude biographique et critique,* Paris, 1867 (3rd edition, enlarged, 1879); F. H. Lem, "Géricault portraitiste," *L'Arte,* Jan.-June, 1963, p. 68

Signed "T.G." at the lower left, this picture was traditionally supposed to be a portrait of the composer F. A. Böieldieu (1775-1834) although it does not bear any very pronounced resemblance to his known portraits. Of unusually tight and careful finish, the portrait is to be considered one of Géricault's master copies, executed probably about 1810-12, after a slightly earlier work by a portraitist in the vicinity of Boilly or the elder Isabey. Other, equally deceptive copies by him are known (e.g. the copy after H. Rigaud's *Portrait of the Mother of the Artist,* private collection, Paris).

8 Camille COROT (1796-1875)

Harvester Under Trees, ca. 1829
Oil on canvas: 15 13/16" x 12" (40.1 x 30.5 cm.)
Lower left: Stamp, Vente Corot

Collections: M. Mauritz, Paris; Adrien Meunier, Paris; Galerie Daber, Paris

Exhibitions: See catalog ref. page
First Exhibited: I
Not Exhibited: X, XXIII

Literature: Alfred Robaut, *L'Oeuvre de Corot,* Paris: H. Floury, 1905, vol. II, p. 74, no. 219 bis, vol. IV, p. 230, no.323 bis, (sketch by A. Robaut from Posthumous Sale Catalog Hôtel Drouot, May 26, 1875); François Daulte, "Hammer en dix chefs-d'oeuvre," *Connaissance des Arts,* Sept. 1970, pp. 82-83, repr. in color

---

Executed at about the same time as the Hammer *Medieval Ruins* and in a similar rapid style, this picture is considerably darker in tonality and for that reason more suggestive of the work of the Barbizon school. Only the harvester's white shirt and the light patch of sky relieve the rich greens and browns of the shadows. The serpentine wall connecting foreground and middleground and the diagonally recessive row of trees are unusual devices for Corot. They provide a somewhat more obvious pictorial scaffolding than one finds in the painter's later work. The subject is a scene of unposed action, also unusual for Corot.

9 Camille COROT (1796-1875)

Medieval Ruins, ca. 1828-1830
Oil on canvas, mounted on board: 9" x 12" (23.0 x 30.5 cm.)
Lower right: Stamp, Vente Corot; red wax seal of the Vente Corot, verso

Collections: Vente Corot, 1875, no. 329; Comte Armand Doria (Sale, Paris, May 5, 1899, no. 108); Madame Lazard,

Paris; Mr. and Mrs. Eliot Hodgkin, London (Sale, London, Sotheby & Co., Apr. 29, 1964, no. 35A repr.); Norton Simon, Los Angeles (Sale, New York, Parke-Bernet Galleries, Inc., May 5, 1971, no. 2, repr.)

Exhibited: Paris, Musée Jacquemart-André, *Le Second Empire,* 1957, no. 62; Chicago, The Art Institute, *Corot,* 1960, no. 23; London, Marlborough Fine Art, Ltd., *Corot,* 1963 no. 10

Exhibitions: See catalog ref. page
First Exhibited: IX
Not Exhibited: XXIII

Literature: Alfred Robaut, *L'Oeuvre de Corot,* Paris: H. Floury, 1905, vol. II, p. 75, no. 212, repr.; Sale catalog, *Impressionist and Modern Paintings, Drawings and Sculpture,* London: Sotheby & Co., Apr. 29, 1964, no. 35A, repr.; Sale catalog, *Highly Important 19th and 20th Century Paintings, Drawings & Sculpture from the Private Collection of Norton Simon,* New York: Parke-Bernet Galleries, Inc., May 5, 1971, no. 2, repr.

Catalogued in the Vente Corot as "Pierrefonds, au pied du Chateau," this picture has been said by Robaut to be a view of Arques-la-Bataille. The latter site, near Dieppe, contains the ruins of an eleventh-century fortress built by an uncle of William the Conqueror. The former, near Compiègne, was the site of a fourteenth-century chateau, the remains of which were completely rebuilt by Viollet-le-Duc in the mid-nineteenth century at the order of Napoleon III. Robaut lists two views of Arques painted by Corot about the time of this sketch, three drawings and two paintings of Pierrefonds. Of the latter, three were executed in the 1840's and two in the 1860's. The present picture was probably painted between Corot's first two trips to Italy, that is about 1828-1830. It combines his interest in subjects observed on the spot with the luminism he had developed in the south. In this case the evenness of the northern French light produces two large tonal areas, a light sky and a darker foreground, forecasting the softness of Corot's late work and contrasting with the sharper illumination of his Italian pictures.

10 Camille COROT (1796-1875)

Distant View of Mantes Cathedral, ca. 1855-1860
Oil on canvas: 22 1/16" x 18 1/16" (56.0 x 45.9 cm.)
Signed lower left: Corot

Collections: M. Knoedler & Co., Paris, 1899; Galerie Georges Petit, Paris (Sale, Paris, Hôtel Drouot, Apr. 27, 1933, no. 49); M. Damidot; Ferdinand Blumenthal, Paris; Léfèvre

Gallery, London; Count Pecci-Blunt, Paris; C. W. Boise, London

Exhibited: Paris, Galerie Georges Petit, Exposition Vingt Peintures du XIXe Siècle, Cent Chefs-d'Oeuvre de l'Ecole Française, 1910, no. 8; New York, M. Knoedler & Co., The Landscape in French Painting, XIXth-XXth Centuries, 1910; Amsterdam, Les Peintures Françaises aux XIXème et XXème Siècles, April-May, 1931

Exhibitions: See catalog ref. page
First Exhibited: I
Not Exhibited: XXIII

Literature: Alfred Robaut, *L'Oeuvre de Corot,* Paris: H. Floury, 1905, vol. II, p. 264, no. 818, repr. p. 265; L. Roger-Miles, *Chefs-d'Oeuvre de l'Ecole Française,* Paris: Georges Petit, 1911, repr. p. 103; Horace Shipp, *The French Masters,* London: Samson Low, Marston & Co., repr. p. 112; *Gazette des Beaux-Arts, Apr. 21, 1933, repr. p. 3; Gazette des Beaux-Arts,* May 5, 1933, p. 6; *Art News,* Apr. 8, 1933, repr. p. 8; Germain Bazin, *Corot,* Paris, 1950, pl. 92; Radolphe Walter, "Jean Baptiste Corot et la Cathédrale Restaurée," *Gazette des Beaux-Arts,* Apr. 1966, pp. 217-228, repr.; *Burlington Magazine,* Apr. 1968, repr. p. VII; *Connoisseur,* Aug. 1968, repr. p. XIV; Sale catalog, *Impressionist and Modern Paintings, Drawings and Sculpture—Various Owners,* London: Sotherby & Co., Apr. 24, 1968, no. 61, repr.

Mantes (Mantes-la-jolie), a small town east of Paris notable for its magnificent church designed by Eudas de Montreuil, architect of Nôtre Dame at Paris, was painted many times by Corot between the early 1840's and the 1860's. He particularly favored its church and the bridge across the Seine as motifs. The present picture is not dissimilar to one in Reims taken from a slightly different viewpoint (Robaut 1522) although the composition is stronger by virtue of the placement of the trees and the log lying in the foreground. Two drawings in horizontal format (Robaut 817, 1519) were apparently made from the same spot. The disproportion in the towers of the church has led Walter to point out that the painting must have been executed during the rebuilding of the south tower from 1859-1860. He convincingly suggests that it dates to May 1859 when Corot was at nearby Rosny. The tonality of the picture is somewhat lighter and more even than one is used to from Corot, although he has been careful to add his usual small touch of red to spark the blue-green of the overall composition.

11 Camille COROT (1796-1875)

Portrait of a Girl, ca. 1860
Oil on canvas: 12 1/4″ x 9 3/16″ (32.1 x 24.3 cm.)
Signed upper right: Corot

Collections: Emile Bernheim, Paris, André Pacitti, Paris

Exhibitions: See catalog ref. page
First Exhibited: IV
Not Exhibited: XXIII

Literature: André Schoeller and Jean Dieterle, *Corot Deuxième Supplément à "L'Oeuvre de Corot" par Alfred Robaut et Moreau-Nélaton, Editions Floury,* Paris: Quatre Chemins, 1956, no. 28

———————————

Degas was amoung the first to appreciate Corot's abilities as a figure painter, abilities that have generally gone unrecognized because of the popularity of the artist's landscapes. Toward the end of his life Corot's figures became generalized into national or allegorical types, and individualized portraits such as this became increasingly rare. During the same period the artist showed a marked predilection for a Leonardesque type, its softly-modeled face gazing abstractedly outward, its arms folded across each other. The Louvre's *Woman with the Pearl* is the best example of this type, and the 1962 *Figures de Corot* catalog suggests a relationship with both the *Mona Lisa* and the *Belle Ferronnière.* A portrait of a young woman from the Hirschland Collection represents an intermediate compositional step between the *Woman with the Pearl* and this picture.

12 Camille COROT (1796-1875)

Morning
Oil on canvas: 69 11/16″ x 52 3/8″ (177.0 x 133.0 cm.)
Signed lower left: Corot

Collections: M. Larrieu, Bordeaux; E. Secrétan (Sale, July 1, 1889, no. 2)

Exhibited: Paris, *Salon of 1865,* no. 506, under the title: *Le Matin;* Paris, Ecole des Beaux-Arts, 1875, no. 148 (lent by M. Larrieu, Bordeaux); Paris, Arnold & Tripp, Feb. 1883

Exhibitions: See catalog ref. page
First Exhibited: II
Not Exhibited: X, XX, XXIII

Literature: Alfred Robaut, *L'Art,* Paris, Feb. 18, 1883; Alfred Robaut, *L'Oeuvre de Corot,* Paris: H. Floury, 1905, vol. III, no. 1635, repr. p. 145; Etienne Moreau-Nélaton, *Corot, raconté par lui-même,* Paris: Henri Laurens, 1924, vol. II, fig. 191

———————————

Seeing this picture in the Salon of 1865 Paul Mantz wrote, "No landscape is as fresh, as tender, as bathed in the dawn as *Morning,"* and in 1883, Alfred Robaut, decrying the small number of Corot paintings in French public collections, unsuccessfully demanded that the state allot one hundred thousand francs for its purchase. Robaut maintained that the composition had resulted from Corot's experience of an early morning in the country at Isigny and that a sketch made on the spot (Robaut 846) was preparatory to it. The sketch, however, bears only slight resemblance to the final composition. Of unusual importance because of its size, *Morning* combines Corot's favorite motifs of classical figures and a dark but luminous setting seen against the light. The touch of red in the hair ribbon of the Bacchante is typical of him. The darkening of the picture in the century since it was painted somewhat obscures the original transparency of the coloring. The work has been known variously as *Morning, Bacchame,* and *Bacchante Detaining an Amoretto.*

13   Camille COROT (1796-1875)

Pleasures of Evening
Oil on canvas: 44 1/2″ x 65 3/16″ (113.0 x 165.6 cm.)
Signed and dated lower left: Corot 1875

Collections: Jay Gould, New York; Edwin J. Gould, New York

Exhibitions: See catalog ref. page
First Exhibited: I
Not Exhibited: X, XX, XXIII
Exhibited: Paris, *Salon of 1875,* no. 520; Paris, *Exposition Universelle Internationale de 1878,* no. 201; New York, American Art Galleries, *Exhibition of the Works of Antoine Barye and also Paintings by his Contemporaries and Friends, for the Benefit of the Barye Monument Fund,* Nov. 15, 1889-Jan. 15, 1890, no. 169 (lent by Jay Gould)

Literature: *Salon de 1875, 92° Exposition Officielle,* Paris: Imprimerie Nationale, 1875, p. 77, no. 520; A. de la Fizelière, *Memento du Salon de Peinture, de Gravure, et des Sculptures en 1875,* Paris: Librairies des Bibliophiles, 1875, pp. 32, 65, no. 520; Paul Leroi, "Salon de 1875," *L'Art,* vol. II, XV, p. 269, repr. in lithograph: *L'Exposition de l'Oeuvre de Corot* (biographical note by P. Burty), Paris: 1875, p. 31; Anatole de Montaiglon, "Salon de 1875," *Gazettes des Beaux Arts,* 2nd series, vol. 12, p. 23; P. de la Flécherye, "Le Salon de 1875," *Le Monde,* Paris: Imprimerie Balitout, Questroy et Cie, 1875, p. 96; Henri Dumesnil, *Corot, Souvenirs Intimes,* Paris: Rapilly, 1875, pp. 102, 130, no. 120; *L'Alliance des Lettres et des Arts,* Apr. 1, 1875, repr. in pen drawing; *L'Univers Illustré,* May 1, 1875, repr. in woodcut; Jules Claretie, *L'Art et les Artistes Français Contemporains, Salon de 1875,* Paris: Charpentier et Cie, 1876, p. 356; *Catalogue Officiel de l'Exposition Universelle Internationale de 1878 à Paris,* Paris: Imprimerie Nationale, 1878, vol. I, section I

(Oeuvres d'Art), p. 20, no. 201; *Exposition Universelle Internationale de Paris, 1878, Le Livre d'Or des Exposants,* Paris: André Sagnier, 1878, p. 8; Paul Mantz, "L'Art Moderne à l'Exposition de 1878, La Peinture Française," *Gazette des Beaux Arts,* Paris: A. Quantin, 1879, p. 24; Jules Claretie, "C. Corot," *Peintres et Sculpteurs Contemporains,* lst series, Paris, 1882, pp. 97-120; J. Castagnary, *Salons, 1857-1879,* Paris: Charpentier et Cie, 1892, vol. II, p. 41; *Corot and Millet, with Critical Essays by Gustave Geffroy and Arsène Alexandre,* London and New York: Offices of *The Studio,* 1902, p. CXXVIII; Etienne Moreau-Nélaton, *Histoire de Corot et de Ses Oeuvres,* Paris: H. Floury, 1905, fig. 260, pp. 342, 359; Alfred Robaut, *L'Oeuvre de Corot,* Paris: H. Floury, 1905, vol. I, p. 333, vol. III, pp. 322-323, no. 2195, repr., vol. IV, pp. 170, 278, 378, table p. 34; Etienne Moreau-Nélaton, *Corot, raconté par lui-même,* Paris: Henri Laurens, 1924, fig. 258, pp. 89, 105, repr. p. 175; Germain Bazin, *Corot,* Paris: Editions Pierre Tisné, 1951 (2nd ed.), p. 115; Daniel Band-Bovy, *Corot,* Geneva: Alexandre Julien, 1957, p. 251; *Apollo,* May 1967, p. LXXIV, repr.

Castagnary wrote of this picture and the *Woodcutters,* both exhibited posthumously in the Salon of 1875, that they were "worthy of the most beautiful among their predecessors." Among the last of Corot's paintings, *Pleasures of Evening* repeats the theme of an antique dance in the forest that he had treated more than once before. Begun at Courbron, a small town just east of Paris where Corot was in the habit of visiting friends and working toward the end of his life, the picture was finished in Paris. Between its inception and its completion it was sketched by Robaut (2195 [A]). It is clear from the sketch that Corot made several changes after his return to Paris, apparently reworking the figures in the group at right center and adding the two figures at the left.

14   Honoré DAUMIER (1808-1879)

The Lawyers (The Bar) circa 1860
Oil on canvas, 12 9/16″ x 19 3/4″ (32.5 x 50 cm.)
Signed lower right

Collections: Corot, Geoffroy-Dechaume, Bureau

Exhibited: Paris 1878, *Durand-Ruel,* no. 39; Paris 1888, *La Caricature,* no. 34; Paris 1900, *Exposition Internationale Universelle,* no. 186; Paris 1901, *Beaux-Arts,* no. 17

Exhibitions: See catalog ref. page
First Exhibited: XXXV

Literature: *Catalogue de la vente, Collection Particulière Corot,* Paris 1875, no 664; *Alexandre* pp. 355/56 and 375; *Catalogue de la vente, Geoffroy-Dechaume,* Paris 1893, no 23; Klossowski

110; *Catalogue de la vente P. Bureau,* Paris 1927, no 98; *L'Amour de l'Art,* 1927, p. 155; Fuchs 20b; *Eschollier* 1930, pl. 19; *Scheiwiller,* pl. XX; *Roger-Marx,* p. 30; *Feischmann/Sachs,* pl. 21; *Adhémar,* pl. 127.

(Excerpt from the book by K. E. Maison)

Alexandre tells a charming story about Gambetta's comments, when the famous statesman - once a lawyer himself - saw the painting at the exhibition held at the Galerie Durand-Ruel in 1878. Gambetta claimed that in the painting he recognized several of his onetime colleagues, but Geoffroy Dechaume, who accompanied Gambetta, alleged that Daumier had not set foot in a law-court for the last ten years, and that these were mere creatures of his imagination, and not actual people, but the prototype of the "Lawyer" as seen by Daumier .... "He knows lawyers better than they do themselves. That is why the resemblance seems so striking."

15 Eugène BOUDIN (1824-1898)

Beach at Trouville
Oil on canvas: 12 7/8″ x 7 5/16″ (32.7 x 18.6 cm.)
Signed lower right: a M^ns Sonnerville (sic)
Souvenir de E. Boudin
Inscribed lower left: Trouville

Collections: de Sonnerville, Bordeaux; Hallsborough, London; Lock Galleries, New York

Exhibitions: See catalog ref. page
First Exhibited: I
Not Exhibited: XX, XXIII
Literature: *Art News, Feb. 1967, repr. p. 53*

The horizontal format of this sketch and frieze-like arrangement of people midway in the composition are characteristic of Boudin's beach scenes. This one was taken at Trouville, one of his favorite haunts and among the most fashionable of the Second Empire resorts.

16 Eugène BOUDIN (1824-1898)

Sailing Ships in Port
Oil on canvas: 17 3/4″ x 25 5/16″ (45.1 x 64.3 cm.)
Signed and dated lower left: E. Boudin 1869

Collection: Allard et Nöel, Paris

Exhibitions: See catalog ref. page
First Exhibited: I
Not Exhibited: XX, XXIII

Descended from Seventeenth-Century Holland by way of Eighteenth-Century Venetian *vedute,* Boudin's paintings contrast towering, broadly-brushed skies with more precisely-rendered, flickering groups of figures, ships, and buildings stretched out along the horizon. The precision of their naturalistic observation and their narrow tonal range of grayed blue, green, and ochre sparked with occasional accents of red attracted the attention of the young Impressionists, most notably that of Monet. In 1869, the year of this picture, Boudin wrote of "the sundrenched beaches and the stormy skies, and of the joy of painting them in the sea breezes."

17 Eugène BOUDIN (1824-1898)

Quay at Camaret
Oil on canvas: 14 1/2″ x 23″ (36.8 x 58.4 cm.)
Signed and dated lower left: Boudin '73
Inscribed lower right: Camaret

Collections: Bernheim-Jeune, Paris; L. Bernard; Théodore Révillon, Paris; Georges Petit, Paris; Galerie Schmit, Paris

Exhibitions: See catalog ref. page
First Exhibited: I
Not Exhibited: XX, XXIII

In 1872 and 1873 Boudin worked at Camaret, at the extreme western tip of Brittany. This picture, somewhat stronger in its tonal contrasts than is common for him, seems almost an illustration of Gustave Geffroy's statement that "Eugène Boudin is one of the immediate precursors of Impressionism....He has perceived that opaque black does not exist, and that air is transparent. He observes the value that objects acquire when exposed to light, and how planes fall into place and lead to the horizon." Boudin himself, constantly conscious of the gap between his perceptions and his expressive powers, wrote, "Sometimes, as I walk sunken in melancholy, I look at the light inundating the earth, trembling on the water, playing on clothing, and I become faint when I realize how much genius is needed to grasp so many difficulties."

18 Gustave MOREAU (1826-1898)

Salome, 1876
Oil on canvas: 56 5/8″ x 41 1/16″ (143.8 x 104.2 cm.)

Collections: Louis Mante, Marseilles (Sale, Paris, Galerie Charpentier, Nov. 28, 1956, no. 10); Robert Lebel, Paris; Julius Weitzner, London, 1958; Huntington Hartford, New York

Exhibited: Paris, *Salon of 1876,* no. 1506; Paris, *Exposition Universelle Internationale, 1878,* no. 659; Paris, Galeries Georges Petit, *Gustave Moreau Exposition au Profit des*

Oeuvres du Travail et des Pauvres Honteux, 1906, no. 76, (lent by Louis Mante); Paris, Musée du Louvre, *Gustave Moreau,* June, 1961, no. 22 (lent by Huntington Hartford); New York, Museum of Modern Art, Dec. 4, 1961-Feb. 4, 1962, and Chicago, Illinois, Art Institute of Chicago, Mar.2-Apr. 15, 1962, *Odilon Redon—Gustave Moreau—Rudolphe Bresdin,* no. 177 (lent by Huntington Hartford)

Exhibitions: See catalog ref. page
First Exhibited: IX
Not Exhibited: XX, XXVII, XXIX
Exhibited: Los Angeles, Los Angeles County Museum of Art, *Moreau Exhibition,* July 23-Sept. 1, 1974; San Francisco, Palace of the Legion of Honor, *Moreau Exhibition,* Sept. 14-Nov. 3, 1974

Literature: *Salon de 1876, Palais de Champs Elysées, Explication des Ouvrages,* Paris: Imprimerie Nationale, May 1, 1876, no. 1506, p. 187; P. deSaint Victor, *La Liberté,* May 19, 1876; *Zigzags, Salon de 1876, Gustave Moreau,* June 25, 1876 no. 9, p. 2; Charles Yriarte, "Le Salon de 1876," *Gazette des Beaux-Arts,* Paris: Imprimerie Nationale, 6th ed., vol. 13, pp. 705-708, p. 698, repr. (sketch for *Salome*); Pierre de Savarus, *Le Salon de 1876, à Vol d'Oiseau,* Paris: Chez Dentu, 1876, pp. 43, 44; Georges Dufour, "Le Grande Art et le Petit Art du Salon de 1876," *L'Artiste,* Amiens: Typographie Delattre-Lenoel, pp. 24, 25; Victor deSwarte, *Lettres sur le Salon de 1876,* Saint Omer: Imprimerie Fleury-LeMaire, 1876, p. 79; *Catalogue Officiel de l'Exposition Universelle Internationale de 1878 à Paris,* published by the Commissariat General, Paris: Imprimerie Nationale, vol. I, section I (Oeuvres d'Art), no. 657, p. 51; Paul Mantz, "Paris Exposition Universelle, La Peinture Française," *Gazette des Beaux-Arts,* vol. I, Dec. 1, 1878, p. 47; Charles L. Duval, *Les Beaux-Arts d'l'Exposition de 1878, Impression et Notes d'Artistes,* Meaux: Librairie Ch. Cochet, 1878, p. 127 (from *Le Publicateur,* Arrondissemont de Meaux); *Exposition Universelle de Paris, 1878, Le Livre d'Or des Exposants,* Section I (Beaux-Arts), Paris: André Sagnier, 1878, p. 10; Hippolyte Gautier and Adrien Desprez, *Les Curiosités de l'Exposition de 1878,* Paris: Librairie Charles Delagrave, 1878, p. 87; *Les Artistes Français à l'Exposition Universelle de 1878,* Paris: Georges Décaux, ed., p. 56; M. E. Bergerat, *Les Chefs-d'oeuvre d'Art à l'Exposition Universelle, 1878,* Paris: Ludovic Baschet, 1878, p. 156, repr. pl. 20 (photogravure Goupil et Cie); Paul Mantz, "L'Art Moderne à l'Exposition de 1878," *Gazette des Beaux-Arts,* Paris: A. Quantin, 1879, pp. 31, 33; Pierre de Savarus, *Dix Années d'Art (Souvenir des Expositions),* Paris: 1879, pp. 89-91; Dubosc de Pesquidoux, *L'Art dans les Deux Mondes—Peinture et Sculpture, L'Art au XIXème Siècle,* Paris: E. Plon et Cie, 1881, vol. I, no. IV, p. 82; J.K. Huysman, *A Rebours,* 1884, pp. 71-76; Paul Leprieur, *L'Artiste,* 1889, Mar.: pp. 175, 177, 180, May: pp. 339, 350, 351, June: pp. 444, 449, 450, 452; Jules-Antoine Castagnary, *Salons,* Paris, 1892, vol. II, pp. 227-228; Gustave Larroumet, *Etudes de Littérature et*

d'Art, Paris: 1896, pp. 227-228; *Léon Thévenin, L'Esthétique de Gustave Moreau,* Paris: Vanier, 1897, pp. 9, 12-13; Gleeson White, "The Pictures of Gustave Moreau," *The Pageant,* London: 1897, p. 11; Léonce Bénédite, "Deux Idéalistes, Gustave Moreau et E. Burne-Jones," *La Revue de l'Art Ancien et Moderne,* Apr. 1899, pp. 265-290, p. 273, repr.; Ary Renan, "Gustave Moreau," *Gazette des Beaux-Arts,* Paris: Imprimerie Georges Petit, 1900, pp. 62, 63, repr. (heliogravure by J. Chauvet); Gustave Geffroy, *La Vie Artistique,* 6th series, chap. XVI, Paris: H. Floury, 1900, pp. 143-147; Henri-Frantz, "The New Gustave Moreau Gallery," *Magazine of Art,* 1900, pp. 99-104; Gustave Larroumet, Institut de France, Académie des Beaux-Arts, *Notice Historique sur la Vie et les Oeuvres de M. Gustave Moreau,* Paris: Firmin-Didot et Cie. 1901, pp. 21, 22, 29, 30, repr. p. 36; Musée National Gustave Moreau, *Principales Oeuvres de Maître dans les Musées et Collections Particulières* (intro. Georges Desvallières), Paris: J.E. Bulloz, 1906, no. 9 (heliogravure by J. Chauvet; Mante Coll.); Gustave Geffroy, *L'Oeuvre d'Art, L'Oeuvre de Gustave Moreau,* Paris: Imprimerie L. Lambert, 1906, pp. 5, 9, 26, 27; Catalog, Galerie Georges Petit, *Exposition Gustave Moreau, Au Profit des Oeuvres de Travail et des Pauvres Honteux* (préface, Robert de Montesquiou), Paris: Imprimerie Georges Petit 1906, no. 76, p. 38 (Mante Coll., Marseilles); Arthur Symons, *Studies in Seven Arts,* London: 1910, pp. 73-77; Léon Deshairs and Jean Laran, *L'Art de Notre Temps, Gustave Moreau,* Paris: Librairie Centrale des Beaux-Arts, 1913, pl. XXVIII, pp. 71, 72, repr. opp.; Musée National Gustave Moreau, *L'Oeuvre de Gustave Moreau* (intro. Georges Desvallières), Paris: Bulloz, 1913, no. 9, repr.; Anonymous, *Gustave Moreau (Les Peintres Illustrés,* no. 55), Paris: Pierre Lafitte, 1914, pp. 69-70; *Lettres de Georges Rouault et André Suarès, Gustave Moreau, L'Art et Les Artistes,* no. 66, Apr. 1926, Paris: Armand Dayot, p. 223 repr.; Sale catalog, *Catalogue de la Vente Collection Louis Mante,* Galerie Charpentier, Nov. 28, 1956, Paris: Imprimerie M. Schiffer, no. 10, pl. III; Joris-Karl Huysmans, *Against Nature* (translation of *A. Rebours,* 1884, by Robert Baldick), Baltimore: Penguin, 1959, pp. 63-67; Ragnar von Holten, *L'Art Fantastique de Gustave Moreau,* Paris: Jean Jacques Pauvert, 1960, pp. 19, 20, pl. III, p. 27, repr. in color: Musée du Louvre, *Catalogue de l'Exposition Gustave Moreau,* Paris: Editions des Musées Nationaux, June 1961, no. 22, p. 22, pl. II (Huntington Hartford Coll.); Ragnar von Holten, "Le développement du personnage de Salomé à travers les dessins de Gustave Moreau," *L'Oeil,* Aug. 1961, pp. 44-51, 72; John Rewald, Doré Ashton, and Harold Joachim, *Odilon Redon—Gustave Moreau—Rudolphe Bresdin,* the Museum of Modern Art in collaboration with the Art Institute of Chicago, New York: Doubleday & Co., Inc., 1962, no. 177, p. 116; John Simon, "The Torments of Imagination," *Arts,* Feb. 1962, pp. 20-27, repr.; Daniel Grojnowski, "Les Mystères Gustave Moreau," *Revue Générale des Publications Françaises et Etrangères,* Mar. 1963, vol. 19, no. 190, Editions de Minuit pp. 225-238 (p. 237: sketch); *Catalogue of Paintings from the*

Huntington Hartford Collection in the Gallery of Modern Art, New York: The Foundation for Modern Art, Inc., 1964, no. 14, repr. in color; Ragnar von Holten, *Gustave Moreau, Symbolist,* Stockholm: Natur och Kultur, 1965, pp. 48-65, repr. p. 49; Max Gérard, *Dali,* New York: Harry N. Abrams, 1968, no. 169, detail repr. in color; Sale catalog: *Important Impressionist and Modern Paintings and Drawings,* New York: Parke-Bernet Galleries, Inc., Mar. 10, 1971, no. 29, p. 52, repr. in color

---

The best-known version of the artist's best-known subject, *Salome,* represents the full flower of the tendency toward accumulation in Moreau's art as well as the apotheosis of one of the most notable and hermetic tendencies in late Nineteenth-Century French art and literature. This tendency, which involved a slightly overripe enumerative presentation in both visual and verbal media, culminated in, and was transformed by, the work of Marcel Proust. More than one hundred related drawings are known for Moreau's *Salome* and its variant, *The Apparition,* of which the finished watercolor, now in the Louvre, was also exhibited in the Salon of 1876. The figure of Salome herself was studied in a wooden lay figure covered with wax and dressed, one of the dozen or so surviving pieces of sculpture by Moreau. Holten believes the subject to have been inspired by Flaubert's *Salammbô,* while Duthuit traces it to Mallarmè's *Hérodiade,* but perhaps no specific source is needed for this theme of the *belle dame sans merci* (cf. Mario Praz, *The Romantic Agony)* so common to the fin de siècle. Daffner has pointed out that Moreau's interpretation of the Orpheus myth, the poet's severed head lying on a lyre, is closely related to the Salome theme (*Salome,* Munich, 1912, p. 289). The scene takes place under the surveillance of the Ephesian Artemis in a fantastic architecture of Moorish inspiration. J.K. Huysmans, who placed the painting in the possession of Des Esseintes, hero of *A Rebours,* described Salome as folllows: "Her face composed, solemn, almost august, she begins the lascivious dance which must awaken the deadened senses of the aged Herod....Concentrating, her eyes fixed like those of a sleepwalker, she sees neither the trembling Tetrarch nor her mother, the fierce Herodiade, who watches her, nor the hermaphrodite, or eunuch, who stands, sword in hand, at the foot of the throne." Moreau himself described Salome as, "That woman nonchalantly strolling...in the gardens recently stained by that horrible murder which terrified the executioner himself." Kaplan has called this picture, which has been known variously as *Salome,* the *Dance of Salome,* and *Salome Dancing Before Herod,* Moreau's "most successful synthesis of precise delineation and free handling of oil pigment."

19 Gustave MOREAU (1826-1898)

King David
Oil on canvas: 90 9/16" x 54 5/16" (230.0 x 137.0 cm.)

Collections: Comtesse Roederer, Paris; Hector Brame, Paris; Walter P. Chrysler, Jr., New York

Exhibited: Paris, *Exposition Universelle Internationale,* 1878, no. 659; Toronto, Ontario, The Art Gallery of Ontario, *The Sacred and Profane in Symbolist Art,* Nov. 1969, no. 64; New York, Spencer A. Samuels & Co., Ltd. *Symbolists,* Nov. 1970, no. 116

Exhibitions: See catalog ref. page
First Exhibited: VIII
Not Exhibited: X, XX, XXIII, XXVIII, XXIX
Exhibited: Los Angeles, Los Angeles County Museum of Art, *Moreau Exhibition,* July 23-Sept. 1, 1974; San Francisco, California Palace of the Legion of Honor, *Moreau Exhibition,* Sept. 14-Nov. 3, 1974

Literature: Dubosc de Pesquidoux, *L'Art dans les Deux Mondes, L'Art du XIXème Siècle, Peinture et Sculpture,* Paris: E. Plon et Cie, 1881, vol. l, No. VI, p. 84; Léon Deshairs, *L'Art de Notre Temps, Gustave Moreau,* Paris: Librairie Central des Beaux-Arts, no. XXXIII, pp. 79-80, repr. opp.; *Catalogue de l'Exposition Universelle Internationale,* Paris: Commissariat Général, Imprimerie Nationale, 1878, vol. 1, (Oeuvres d'Art), no. 659, p. 51; "L'Art Moderne à l'Exposition de 1878," *Gazette des Beaux-Arts,* Paris: A. Quantin, 1879, pp. 31-33; Pierre de Savarus, *Dix Années d'Art (Souvenir des Expositions),* Paris: 1879, pp. 94-95; Claude Phillips, "Gustave Moreau," *Magazine of Art,* 1885, pp. 228-233, repr.; Paul Leprieur, "Gustave Moreau et Son Oeuvre," *L'Artiste,* Paris: Mar.-June 1889, p. 40; Jean Lorrain, Sensations et Souvenirs, Paris: 1895, p. 67; Ary Renan, *Gustave Moreau,* Paris: Imprimerie Georges Petit, 1900, pp. 71-73, repr. (etching by M. Bracquemond); Henri Frantz, "The New Moreau Gallery," *The Magazine of Art,* London: Cassell & Co., Ltd., 1900, pp. 97-104, repr. p. 98 (engraving by Jonnard reprinted from Claude Phillips, "Gustave Moreau." *The Magazine of Art,* 1885, pp. 228-233); Gustave Larroumet, Institut de France, Académie des Beaux-Arts, *Notices Historiques sur la Vie et les Oeuvres de M. Gustave Moreau,* Paris: Firmin-Didot et Cie, 1901, p. 36; *Catalogue Sommaire des Peintures, Dessins, Cartons et Aquarelles du Musée Gustave Moreau,* Paris: Imprimeries Réunies, 1902, pp. 9, 22, 33, 49, 50, 55, 113; Louis Dimier, L'Inspiration de Gustave Moreau," *Minerva,* no. 18, Paris: Nov. 15, 1902, p. 126; Camille Mauclair, "The Gustave Moreau Museum in Paris," *The Art Journal,* London: 1905, p. 255, repr. Musée Nationale de Gustave Moreau, *Principales Oeuvres de Maître dans les Musées et Collections Particulières* [(préface, Georges Desvallières). Paris; J. E. Bulloz, 1906, no. 22 in portfolio (heliograph by J. Chauvet); Jean Laran and Léon Deshairs, "Gustave Moreau," L'Art de

Notre Temps, Paris: 1913, pp. 70-79, pl. XXXII, Anonymous, "Gustave Moreau,"] *Les Peintres Illustrés no. 55*, Paris: Pierre Lafitte, 1914, p. 74; Ragnar van Holten, *L'Art Fantastique de Gustave Moreau*, Paris: Jean-Jacques Pauvert, 1906, pl. 37; Spencer A. Samuels, *Symbolists*, New York: Spencer A. Samuels & Co., Ltd., 1970, no. 116, p. 56, repr.

Originally known simply as *David,* this picture has more recently borne the title, *King David Meditating.* In it one sees that juxtaposition of disparate architectural and decorative elements so dear to Moreau. The cross-decorated temple lamp and the evangelist symbols on the capitals may perhaps indicate a Christian, specifically Catholic, interpretation of David as a prototype of Christ. Further, the painting borders on being an allegory of the senses, with the aged psalmist surrounded by flowers, incense, and a burning lamp and clothed in jewels and rich materials. The subtle rhythms of the asymmetrical composition and the softening of the delicate and intricate detail in a poetic atmosphere distinguish Moreau's salon paintings like the *King David* from the empty formalism and banal sentiments of so many of his academic contemporaries. Of this kind of picture, Ary Renan wrote in the *Gazette des Beaux-Arts* in 1899. "His (Moreau's) idea was to equal, without deranging the harmony of line, and by the prestige alone of environing decorations, all the suggestions provoked in literature, music and the theater."

20 Camille PISSARRO (1830-1903)

Boulevard Montmartre, Mardi Gras
Oil on canvas: 25″ x 31 1/2″ (63.5 x 77.5 cm.)
Signed and dated lower left: C. Pissarro '97

Collections: Maurice Barret-Décap, Paris; Mr. and Mrs. Henry R. Luce, New York; Marlborough Alte und Moderne Kunst, Zurich; Norton Simon, Los Angeles (Sale, New York Parke-Bernet Galleries, May 5, 1971, no. 24, repr.)

Exhibited: Paris, Galerie Durand-Ruel, *C. Pissarro,* 1898, no. 20; Paris, Galerie Durand-Ruel, *Tableaux, Pastels et Gouaches de C. Pissarro,* 1921, no. 9; Paris, Galerie Durand-Ruel, *C. Pissarro,* 1928, no. 78; New Haven, Yale University Art Gallery, *Paintings, Drawings, and Sculpture Collected by Yale Alumni,* May 19-June 26, 1960, no. 58 (repr. in cat.); New York, Wildenstein & Co., Inc., *C. Pissarro,* Mar. 25-May 1, 1965, no. 65 (repr. in cat.)

Exhibitions: See catalog ref. page
First Exhibited: IX
Not Exhibited: XX, XXIII
Exhibited: Pittsburgh, Pennsylvania, Carnegie Institute,

The Sarah Scaife Gallery of the Museum of Art, *Inaugural Celebration Exhibition,* Oct. 26-Dec. 9, 1974

Literature: Ludovic-Rodo Pissarro and Lionello Venturi, *C. Pissarro, Son Art—Son Oeuvre,* 1939, no. 995, repr., vol. II, pl. 200; Sale catalog, *Highly Important 19th and 20th Century Paintings, Drawings and Sculpture from the Private Collection of Norton Simon,* New York: Parke-Bernet Galleries, May 5, 1971, no. 24, p. 40, repr. opp. in color

---

Pissarro produced several paintings of the Boulevard Montmartre in 1897 (Venturi-Pissarro 986-998), three of which (Venturi-Pissarro 995-997) seem to represent successive stages of a Lenten parade. Although the three are surely related, two, including this one, are catalogued by Venturi and Pissarro as Mardi Gras scenes and the third as a Mi-Carême. This picture is characteristic of Pissarro's late interest in city scenes, particularly views of Paris, seen at sharp downward angles. Characteristic too are the blond tonality and obvious feathery or calligraphic brushwork he used toward the end of his life. Partly because of the nature of the subject, this picture has somewhat more color than others of Pissarro's Paris views.

21 Edgar DEGAS (1834-1917)

Three Dancers in Yellow Skirts, ca. 1891
Oil on canvas: 32″ x 25 5/8″ (81.3 x 65.1 cm.)
Signed lower right: Degas

Collections: Atelier Degas (lst Sale, Paris, Galerie Georges Petit, May 6-8, 1918, no. 82, repr.); MM. Nunès and Fiquet, Paris; F. R. (S-le, Paris, Mar. 8, 1920, no. 74); Galerie René Drouet, Paris; Erwin Swann, Pennsylvania (Sale, London, Sotheby & Co., Dec. 10, 1969, no. 20, repr.)

Exhibited: New York, Gallery of Modern Art, *The Pleasure of the Eye—The Collection of Caroline and Erwin Swann, 1964-65,* no. 9; Portland Art Museum; Seattle Art Museum; Salt Lake Art Center; Colorado Springs Fine Arts Center; Kansas City, William Rockhill Nelson Gallery of Art; University of Michigan, Museum of Art; Dayton Art Institute

Exhibitions: See catalog ref. page
First Exhibited: III
Not Exhibited: XX, XXIII

Literature: Sale catalog, *Catalogue des Tableaux, Pastels et Dessins par Edgar Degas,* 2nd sale, Paris: Galerie Georges Petit, 1918, no. 92, p. 51, repr.; Sale catalog, *Catalogue de la Vente F.R.,* Paris; Hôtel Drouot, Mar. 8, 1930, 2nd part, no. 74, p. 20, repr.; P. A. Lemoisne, *Degas et Son Oeuvre,* Paris: 1947, vol. III, p. 636, no. 1100, repr.; Sale catalog,

Impressionist and Modern Paintings, London: Sotheby & Co., Dec. 10, 1969, no. 20, repr. in color

---

This picture is similar in size and conception to the Louvre *Dancers in Blue* which is, in turn, closely related to the Metropolitan Dancers in Red and Green. The Louvre picture and this one seem, in fact, to be coloristic variations on the same theme, the Louvre painting developed in blue-green-purple, this one in red-yellow-orange. The broadly stippled background was explored by Degas in other pictures at this time, both of dancers (Lemoisne 975) and of bathers (Lemoisne 1104). The placement of the figures suggests the same or similar poses seen from different angles of vision, a device increasingly exploited by Degas. Along with his interest in different poses arranged sequentially, the resulting photo-cinematic effect almost certainly reflects his knowledge of early experiments in motion photography. This effect is enhanced by the suggestion of unstable equilibrium resulting from eccentric arrangement of the figures. The entire composition is stabilized by Degas' manipulation of his hues and their values.

22 Henri FANTIN-LATOUR (1836-1904)

Peonies in a Blue and White Vase
Oil on canvas: 23 15/16″ x 19 5/8″ (60.8 x 49.9 cm.)
Signed and dated upper right: Fantin 1872

Collections: Dr. J. van Alphen-Carp. The Netherlands; E.J. van Wisselingh & Co., Amsterdam; M.L. de Boer, Amsterdam

Exhibitions: See catalog ref. page
First Exhibited: I

Literature: Mme. Fantin-Latour, *Catalogue de l'Oeuvre Complete de Fantin-Latour,* Paris: H. Floury, 1911, no. 616; *Art Journal,* Fall 1968, p. LIV, repr.; *Connoisseur,* Nov. 1968, p. 11, repr.; Francois Daulte, "Hammer en dix chefs d'oeuvre," *Connaissance des Arts,* Sept. 1970, p. 83, repr.

Fantin is most widely known for his flower pictures, in the best of which white predominates against a cool-hued background. Seen in isolation, the flowers in these paintings project in astonishing relief and tactility. This heightened sense of reality is partly due to he apparent lack of atmosphere in the flower pieces. Perhaps none of these paintings illustrates as well as this one Jacques-Emile Blanche's observation that "Fantin studied each flower, each petal, its grain, its tissue as if it were a human face....It is an individual flower and not simply one of a type....Some canvases are worthy of Chardin."

23 Henri FANTIN-LATOUR (1836-1904)

Portrait of Miss Edith Crowe
Oil on canvas: 28 3/4″ x 23 5/16″ (73.0 x 59.2 cm.)
Signed and dated upper left: Fantin '74

Collections: Mme. Paul Paix; Mrs. D. Bergen-Hayn; Galerie l'Oeil, Paris

Exhibited: Paris, *Salon of 1875,* no. 783; Paris, Ecole Nationale des Beaux-Arts, *Exposition de l'Oeuvre de Fantin-Latour,* May—June 1906, no. 41; Amsterdam, Stedelijk Museum

Exhibitions: See catalog ref. page
First Exhibited: II
Not Exhibited: X, XX, XXIII

Literature: Ministère de l'Instruction Publique et des Beaux-Arts, *Salon de 1875, 92ème Exposition Officielle,* Paris: Imprimerie Nationale, 1875, p. 115, no. 783; Paul Leroi, *L'Art, Salon de 1875,* Paris: Librairie de l'Art, 1875, vol. i, p. 137, no. 783; Adolphe Julien, *Fantin-Latour, sa vie et ses amitiés,* Paris: Lucien Laveur, 1909, p. 199; Mme. Fantin-Latour, *Catalogue de l'Oeuvre Complète de Fantin-Latour,* Paris: H. Floury, 1911, p. 81, no. 739; *Connoisseur,* Nov. 1970, p. 210, repr.

This picture was exhibited as "portrait of Mlle. E. C...." in the Salon of 1875 along with Fantin's superb double portrait of his English friends and patrons, Mr. and Mrs. Edwin Edwards, to whom he had been introduced by Whistler. Miss Crowe was presumably a friend of the Edwards', or of someone whom they had introduced to Fantin. It has been reported that E. C. was the youngest of a large family that lived in Paris. Apparently her house was like a salon for many of the artists of that time. Broader in technique than Fantin's flower pieces, this picture is not yet as free as the allegories and Wagnerian paintings which are almost pre-Raphaelite in character. The placement of the figure against an unmodulated dark ground suggests what Fantin may owe to Monet, although the head is developed in a more traditional chiaroscuro. Speaking of another of Fantin's portraits, Zola noted that "Each of his canvases is an act of conscience. He excels at painting figures in the atmosphere in which they live, in giving them a warm and supple life; it is that which means that, despite the restraining frame in which it is enclosed, this hardly seems to be a portrait, it is nothing less than a thing apart, very elevated."

24 Henri FANTIN-LATOUR (1836-1904)

Roses
Oil on canvas: 26 1/16" x 22 11/16" (66.2 x 57.7 cm.)
Signed and dated upper left: Fantin '84

Collections: Mrs. Edwards, London; Miss R. Bryant, London;
Arthur Tooth & Sons, Ltd., London; Mrs. Hazel C. Boise,
London (Sale, London, Sotheby & Co., Apr. 26, 1967, no. 7,
repr. p. 14)

Exhibited: Musée de Grenoble, *Exposition du Centenaire de la
Naissance de Fantin-Latour*, Aug.-Oct. 1936, no. 145;
London, Arthur Tooth & Sons, Ltd., *French Pictures from
Private Collections*, June 1949, no. 19

Exhibitions: See catalog ref. page
First Exhibited: I
Not Exhibited: XX, XXIII

Literature: Mme. Fantin-Latour, *Catalogue de l'Oeuvre
Complète de Fantin-Latour*, Paris: H. Floury, 1911,
no. 1167; *Burlington Magazine*, Apr. 1967, p. XVI, repr.;
Connoisseur, Apr. 1967, p. XCIII, repr.; Sale catalog,
Impressionist and Modern Paintings and Sculpture, London:
Sotheby & Co., Apr. 1967, p. 15, no. 7, repr. p. 14

The Mrs. Edwards who originally owned this picture is
presumably Mrs. Edwin Edwards, wife of Fantin's
English friend and patron. Although Fantin's portraits
and genre subjects were favored in France, his flower
pictures were particularly popular in England, and his
submissions to the Royal Academy between 1862 and
1900 consisted almost entirely of such subjects. Many
of these had poetic titles such as, "Here Without a
Thorn, the Rose." Although this picture seems
originally to have been called simply *Roses*, it has been
known as *All the Roses of the Garden*, probably because
of Madame Fantin-Latour's description of it in her
catalog. *Roses* is a "poetic," close-valued, and
somewhat more broadly-brushed painting than the
Hammer *Peonies*, the pastel pinks and yellows mediating
between the white highlights and the deep red and
dark greens to soften the picture's general appearance.
This atmospheric facture is particularly appropriate in
view of the literary associations roses seem regularly
to have evoked in Fantin.

25 Alfred SISLEY (1839-1899)

Timber Yard at Saint-Mammès, 1880
Oil on canvas: 21 1/2" x 28 3/4" (55.6 x 72.9 cm.)
Signed lower right: Sisley

Collections: M. Feder, Paris; Durand-Ruel, Paris (purchased
June 25, 1892); Paul Cassirer, Berlin; Galerie Europe,

Brussels; Sale, London, Sotheby & Co., Nov. 29, 1967,
no. 28, repr. p. 46

Exhibited: Paris, Galerie Durand-Ruel, *Monet, Pissarro,
Renoir et Sisley*, Apr. 1899, no. 136; London, Grafton
Gallery, *Paintings by Boudin, Sisley*, Jan.-Feb. 1905, no. 303;
Paris, Galerie Durand-Ruel, *Sisley*, June 1910, no. 71

Exhibitions: See catalog ref. page
First Exhibited: I
Not Exhibited: XX, XXIII

Literature: Gustave Geffroy, *Sisley*, Paris: G. Crès et Cie,
1923, repr. pl. 10; Gustave Geffroy, *Cahiers d'Aujourd'hui*,
Paris, 1923, vols. 13, 14, pp. 7-30; Gustave Geffroy, *Sisley*,
Paris: G. Crès et Cie, 1927, repr. pl. 28; Gotthard Jedlicka,
Sisley, Bern, 1949, repr. pl. 37; François Daulte, *Alfred
Sisley, Catalogue Raisonné de l'Oeuvre Peint*, Lausanne:
Durand-Ruel, 1959, no. 368, repr. p. 372; Sale catalog,
Impressionist and Modern Paintings, Drawings and Sculpture,
London: Sotheby & Co., Nov. 29, 1967, p. 47, no. 28, repr.
color p. 46; *Burlington Magazine*, Nov. 1967, p. 1 repr.;
Apollo, Nov. 1967, p. CXVIII, repr.; *Art News*, Nov. 1967,
p. 17, repr.; *Apollo*, June 1968, p. CII, repr.; *Connoisseur*,
June 1968, p. XIV, repr.

Sisley was at his best in broad, close-valued, tonal
painting. The typical comma-like Impressionist facture
tended to be disruptive of such painting, and Sisley used
it most effectively when his strokes were of fairly
uniform size and shape and his colors within one or two
narrow ranges of tone, as in this picture. Saint-Mammès,
to which Sisley eventually retired, was a small town on
the banks of the Loing in the area southeast of
Fontainebleau. Daulte lists at least three other
compositions directly related to this (369, 370, 372)
and one of the same scenes from the opposite
direction (371).

26 Paul CEZANNE (1839-1906)

Boy Resting, ca. 1885
Oil on canvas: 21 7/16" x 25 13/16" (54.5 x 65.5 cm.)

Collections: Ambroise Vollard, Paris; Galerie Bernheim-
Jeune, Paris; Galerie Thannhauser, Lucerne; Josef Stransky,
New York; Estate of Josef Stransky (on loan to the Worcester
Art Museum, Worcester, Massachusetts, June 1, 1932-
Mar. 9, 1936); Wildenstein & Co., Inc., New York; Arnold
Kirkeby, New York (Sale, New York, Parke-Bernet Galleries,
Inc., Nov. 19, 1958, no. 16); Mrs. Arnold Kirkeby,
Los Angeles

Exhibited: Paris, Galerie Bernheim-Jeune, *Retrospective Paul
Cézanne*, June 1—30, 1926, no. 5; New York Museum of

Modern Art, *1st Loan Exhibition,* Nov. 1929, no. 13; Chicago, Illinois, Art Institute of Chicago, *A Century of Progress,* June 1-Nov. 1, 1933, no. 318A; Worcester, Massachusetts, Worcester Art Museum, *The Loan Exhibition of the New Museum Building, 1933-1934;* San Francisco, California, California Palace of the Legion of Honor, *French Painting from the 15th Century to the Present Day,* June 8-July 8, 1934, no. 65; Kansas City, Missouri, William Rockhill Nelson Gallery of Art, *Nineteenth Century French Painting,* Mar. 15-Apr. 12, 1936; London, Wildenstein & Co., Ltd., *Collection of a Collector, Modern Painting from Ingres to Matisse, The Private Collection of the Late Joseph Stransky,* July 1936, no. 18; Toledo, Ohio, Toledo Museum of Art, *Cézanne, Gauguin,* Nov. 1-Dec. 13, 1936, no. 29; San Francisco, California, San Francisco Museum of Art, *Paul Cézanne,* Sept. 1-Oct. 4, 1937, no. 16 (repr.); London, Wildenstein & Co., Ltd., *Homage to Paul Cézanne,* July 1939, no. 30; New Haven, Connecticut, Yale University Art Gallery, *Cézanne and the French Tradition,* Jan. 29-Feb. 18, 1945; Cincinnati, Ohio, Cincinnati Art Museum, *Paintings by Paul Cézanne,* Feb. 5-Mar. 9, 1947, no. 4 (repr. pl. 4), (lent by Wildenstein & Co., Ltd.); New York, Wildenstein & Co., Inc., *A Loan Exhibition of Paul Cézanne for the Benefit of the New York Infirmary* (lent by Estate of Josef Stransky), Mar. 27-Apr. 26, 1947, no. 19; Los Angeles, California, Art Galleries, University of California, *California Collects: North and South,* Jan. 20-Feb. 23, 1958, no. 29 (repr.)

Exhibitions: See catalog ref. page
First Exhibited: IX
Not Exhibited: XX, XXIII
Exhibited: Tokyo, Japan, National Museum of Western Art, *Cézanne Exhibition,* Mar. 20-Apr. 19, 1974; Kyoto, Japan, Municipal Museum, *Cézanne Exhibition,* June 1-July 17, 1974; Fukuoka, Japan, Prefectural Cultural Center Museum, *Cézanne Exhibition,* July 24-Aug. 18, 1974

Literature: *Kunst and Künstler,* 1926, XXIV, pp. 448-449; Eugenio d'Ors, *Paul Cézanne,* Paris: Editions des Chroniques du Jour, 1930, p. 25, repr., table: no. VI; *International Studio,* Nov. 1929, p. 66, repr.; Ralph Flint, "The Private Collection of Josef Stransky," *Art News,* May 16, 1931, p. 8, repr.; Perry B. Cott, "The Stransky Collection of Modern Art," *Bulletin of the Worcester Art Museum,* winter 1933, p. 157; Nana Iavorskaïa, *Paul Cézanne,* Milan, 1935, pl. VI; *Parnassus,* Dec. 1936, p. 26, repr., *Art Digest,* Apr. 1, 1936, p. 5, repr.; Maurice Raynal, *Cézanne,* New York, 1936, pl. 51; Lionello Venturi, *Cézanne, Son Art—Son Oeuvre,* Paris: Paul Rosenberg, 1936, vol. I, p. 150, no. 391, vol. II, pl. 107, no. 391, repr.; Ambroise Vollard, *Paul Cézanne, His Life and Art* (trans. Harold L. Van Doren), New York, 1937, pl. 9; *Art News,* Oct. 1958, p. 41, repr.; "Kirkeby Collection at Auction." *Arts,* Nov. 1958, p. 27, repr.; *Connoisseur,* Nov. 1958, p. 124, repr.; Robert Melville, "Exhibitions," *Architectural Review,* Aug. 1959, pp. 131-133, repr.; *Connoisseur,* Jan. 1959, p. 254, repr; *Apollo,* June 1959, p. 215, repr.; Mark Roskill, *Van Gogh,*

Gauguin, and the Impressionist Circle, Greenwich, 1970, p. 231, repr., pl. 179; Elie Faure, *Cézanne,* Paris: Braun & Cie (Collections des Maîtres), n.d., pl. 7; *French Masters of the XIX and XX Century; The Private Collection of J. Stransky, N.Y., including recent accessions up to May 1935* (reprint), New York, n.d., repr.

This picture of a reclining clothed figure, unique in Cézanne's oeuvre, has been known variously as *The Siesta, Boy by the Brook, Reclining Boy,* and *Boy Resting.* Venturi refers to its subject as a peasant, but Vollard is said to have considered it a portrait of the artist's son, Paul. The latter seems not unlikely. It exemplifies as well as any of his paintings the artist's struggle to reconcile pictorial and naturalistic scale and effect. The broad rectilinear paint areas at the top of the canvas were clearly conceived by Cézanne as flat elements directly related to the size and shape of that canvas. Their two-dimensional strength creates a pictorial pressure which jeopardizes the human identity of the figure, makes its location in depth ambiguous, and mitigates its three-dimensionality. That Cézanne could explore such complex problems without sacrificing the quality of his art is an index of his genius.

27 Claude MONET (1840-1926)

View of Bordighera
Oil on canvas: 26" x 32 1/4" (66.0 x 81.9 cm.)
Signed and dated lower left: Claude Monet '84

Collections: Durand-Ruel, Paris; M. Montaignac, Paris; James F. Sutton, New York (Sale, American Art Association of the Plaza Hotel, Jan. 16-17, 1917, no. 143); James B. Hastings, New York; Nils B. Hersloff, Baltimore; Estate of Sigmund N. Hersloff, Baltimore (Sale, New York, Parke-Bernet Galleries, Inc., Oct. 28, 1970, no. 5, p. 8, repr. in color)

Exhibited: Paris, Galerie Georges Petit, *Claude Monet et A. Rodin,* 1889 (lent by M. Montaignac)

Exhibitions: See catalog ref. page
First Exhibited: VII
Not Exhibited: XXIII

Exhibited: New York, Acquavella Galleries, Inc., *Claude Monet Exhibition,* Oct. 26-Nov. 28, 1976

Literature: Theodore Robinson, "Monet," *Modern French Masters, A Series of Biographical and Critical Reviews by American Artists, with 37 Wood Engravings and 28 Half-Tone Illustrations,* by John Charles Van Dyke, wood engraving by Michael Haider, New York: The Century Co., 1896, p. 170;

Apollo, Oct. 1970, p. 141, repr.; *Burlington Magazine,* Oct. 1970, LXXIV, repr.; *Art News,* Oct. 1970, repr.

During the 1880's Monet's palette darkened, a fact which, combined with the discreteness and small size of his brushstrokes and the intensity and value contrasts of his color, tended to give his pictures a woolly texture that is especially noticeable in the Creuse and Belle-Ile paintings. This picture contrasts that roughness with an atmospheric distance and is therefore somewhat less surface-oriented than the similar painting in Chicago. Monet had been attracted to the south on a visit there with Renoir in 1883, and in January of 1884 he returned to paint first at Bordighera on the Italian Riviera, and then at Menton.

28 Berthe MORISOT (1841-1895)

Portrait of "Paule Gobillard"
Niece of Berthe Morisot
Oil on canvas, 28 3/4″ x 23 3/4″ (72.8 x 60.1 cm.)

Collection: Morisot Family

Exhibited: *Berthe Morisot, Exposition Commemorative,* Durand-Ruel, Paris, March 1896, no. 29; *Reunion d'Oeuvres par Berthe Morisot,* Galerie Marcel Bernheim, Paris, June-July 1922, no. 27; *Berthe Morisot,* Malerier, Akvareller og Tegningen, Ny Carlsberg Glypotek, Copenhagen, August-September 1949, no. 37; *Exposition Berthe Morisot,* Musee de Dieppe, Dieppe, July-September 1957, no. 38; *Berthe Morisot Exhibition,* Wildenstein Gallery, New York, November 1960, no. 45

Exhibitions: See catalog ref. page
First Exhibited: XXXV

29 Pierre-Auguste RENOIR (1841-1919)

Grape Pickers at Lunch, ca. 1888
Oil on canvas: 21 7/8″ x 18 1/4″ (55.5 x 46.4 cm.)
Signed lower left: Renoir

Collections: Arsène Alexandre, Paris; Rosenberg & Stiebel, New York

Exhibitions: See catalog ref. page
First Exhibited: II
Not Exhibited: X, XX, XXIII, XXVIII, XXIX

Literature: Sale catalog, Paris: Galerie Georges Petit, May 1903, no. 54

This picture, with its sharp contrasts of hue and its carefully drawn forms, is a product of the mid-1880's — a period of experimentation and reevaluation for Renoir.

He had earlier questioned the validity of recording purely visual impressions, and after studying the Raphael paintings in Rome and the ancient frescoes from Pompeii in the Naples Museum during an Italian trip in 1881-1882, Renoir sought to reassess the importance of drawing, line, modeled form, and compositional reorganization of nature. He even questioned the soundness of painting in the open air directly from nature as opposed to composing in the studio. Like Cézanne, but in his own way, he devoted himself at this time to establishing harmony between Impressionism and the "art of the museums."

The *Grape Pickers at Lunch* is a product of Renoir's exploration of some of these concepts. Instead of his usual soft brushwork, he uses smaller, sharper, more graphic strokes which define and model the figures. Instead of merging his figures with the landscape, as in the Impressionist works of the seventies, he arranges his figures to form a closed concentric group which establishes a real, but limited foreground space, reminiscent of Renaissance "stage-like" space, to which the landscape forms a backdrop.

The probability that the painting is a studio composition is reinforced by the reappearance of the girl with the basket on her back used by Renoir in the *Mussel Gatherers at Berneval,* painted in 1879 and shown in the Salon of 1880. The three girls in the foreground are said to be the daughters of Paul Alexis.

30 Pierre-Auguste RENOIR (1841-1919)

Antibes
Oil on canvas: 25 1/2″ x 32″ (64.8 x 81.3 cm.)
Signed and dated lower right: Renoir '88

Collections: Durand-Ruel, Paris, 1910; Baroness von Brenin, Berlin, 1931; Sale, New York, Parke-Bernet Galleries, Inc. Feb. 25, 1970, no. 21 (repr.)

Exhibited: Paris, Durand-Ruel, *Exposition de Tableaux par Renoir,* Apr. 27-May 15, 1912, no. 5; Akron, Ohio, Akron Art Institute, 1947; Milwaukee, Wisconsin, Milwaukee Art Institute, *Masters of Impressionism,* 1948, no. 38

Exhibitions: See catalog ref. page
First Exhibited: IV
Not Exhibited: XVI, XVII, XVIII, XIX, XX, XXIII, XXVIII, XXIX

Exhibited: Chicago, Illinois, Art Institute of Chicago, *Renoir Exhibition,* Jan. 30-April 1, 1973

Literature: Sale catalog, *Highly Important Impressionist, Post-Impressionist & Modern Paintings and Drawings,* New York: Parke-Bernet Galleries, Inc., Feb. 25, 1970, no. 21, repr. in color

During the 1880's Renoir's efforts to re-study his draftsmanship resulted in a hard and carefully-outlined figure style usually at variance with the continued softness of his backgrounds. Only in the non-figural subjects, such as this view of Antibes, did he maintain and develop his feathery brush style, suppressing contour to an extent which makes the subjects of these pictures seem almost to evaporate. A similar composition is recorded in the collection of Sir Simon and Lady Marks.

31   Pierre-Auguste RENOIR (1841-1919)

Two Girls Reading, 1890-1891
Oil on canvas: 22" x 18 5/8" (55.9 x 47.2 cm.)
Signed lower right: Renoir

Collections: Durand-Ruel, Paris (purchased from Renoir in 1895); H. O. Niethke Gallery, Vienna (purchased 1912); Dr. Herman Eissler, Vienna; Hugo Moser, Heemstede; Mrs. Maria Moser, New York; Dr. and Mrs. Armand Hammer, Los Angeles; Los Angeles County Museum of Art (Gift of Dr. and Mrs. Armand Hammer, 1968)

Exhibited: Zurich, Kunsthaus, 1933; Haarlem, Frans Hals Museum, 1936; Baltimore Museum of Art, Summer 1939; New York, Wildenstein & Co., Inc. *Renoir,* Apr. 8-May 10, 1958, no. 53, p. 67 (repr. in cat.); New York, The Metropolitan Museum of Art, 1959-1967

Exhibitions: See catalog ref. page
First Exhibited: I
Not Exhibited: IV, VI, VII, IX, XXIII
Exhibited: New York, Wildenstein & Co., Inc. *Renoir,* Mar. 27-May 3, 1969, no. 77; Manila, National Museum of Manila, Oct. 2, 1976

Literature: Baltimore Museum of Art *Quarterly,* July 1, 1939, p. 8, repr.; Los Angeles County Museum of Art *Annual Report,* 1968-1969, pp. 18-19, repr.; Alfred Weiner, "Renoir's Daimon," *Arts Magazine,* Apr. 1969, p. 40, repr.; *Gazette des Beaux-Arts,* Feb. 1970, supplement, p. 87, repr.

————————————

This gentle and slightly nostalgic subject is of the kind that most appealed to Renoir and that he was best able to execute successfully. The consistency of the brushwork and warmth of the color help unify the composition, and the painting shows the renewed softness of Renoir's work toward the end of the century. The girl at the left is said to be Julie Manet, daughter of Berthe Morisot and Eugène Manet, while the one at the right is possibly her cousin Paule Gobillard. A less satisfying variation of this composition is recorded in a Scottish private collection (reproduced *Scottish Art Review,* vol. IV, no. 4, 1953, p. 19), and there is also a three-

quarter length variation of a similar subject (reproduced *Beaux-Arts,* Feb. 22, 1935, p. 4).

32   Gustave CAILLEBOTTE (1848-1894)

Square in Argenteuil
Oil on canvas: 23 13/16" x 27 3/4" (60.5 x 70.5 cm.)
Signed lower left: G. Caillebotte

Exhibitions: See catalog ref. page
First Exhibited: V
Not Exhibited: XX, XXIII
Exhibited: Manila, National Museum of Manila, October 2, 1976

Literature: Sale catalog, *Importants Tableaux Modernes,* Paris: Palais Galliéra, June 17, 1970, no. 9

————————————

Known principally as the collector who bequeathed the first great group of Impressionist pictures to the French state, Caillebotte was among the organizers of, and participants in, many of the original Impressionist exhibitions. As a painter, his vision was almost always advanced, and he favored subjects from daily life in natural poses although his execution was often tight and linear to the point of academicism. Caillebotte was at his best in his broadly conceived and freely brushed canvases many of which, like this one, were executed at Argenteuil. This fresh and unexpected work probably dates from the early 1880's.

33   Paul GAUGUIN (1848-1903)

Bonjour M. Gauguin
Oil on canvas, mounted on panel: 29 1/2" x 21 1/2"
(74.9 x 54.6 cm.)
Inscribed lower left: Bonjour M. Gauguin

Collections: Mme. Marie Henry, Le Pouldu; Galerie Barbazanges, Paris; Meyer Goodfriend, New York (Sale, New York; American Art Galleries, Jan. 4-5, 1923, no. 107); B. M. Alexander, New York; Howard Young Galleries, New York; Carlton Mitchell, Annapolis; Count Ivan Pulgoursky, San Antonio; Mrs. Mary Ermolaev, Princeton (Sale, Geneva, Christie, Manson & Woods, Nov. 6, 1969, no. 169, repr.)

Exhibited: Paris Galerie Barbazanges, *Exposition d'Oeuvres Inconnues,* Oct. 10-30, 1919, no. 2; New York, Wildenstein & Co., Inc. *A Retrospective Loan Exhibition for the Benefit of Les Amis de Paul Gauguin and the Penn Normal Industrial and Agricultural School,* Mar. 2-Apr. 18, 1936, no. 14; Montreal, Quebec, Museum of Fine Arts, *Manet to Matisse,* May-June, 1949, no. 14; Paris, Galeries Loize, *Les Amitiés de Monfried et ses reliques de Gauguin,* May 11, 1951, no. 108 (inaugurated by Georges Salles, Director of the Museums of France); Houston, Texas, Museum of Fine Arts, *Paul Gauguin,*

His Place in the Meeting of East and West, Mar. 27-
Apr. 25, 1954, no. 15; Wichita Falls, Texas, The Museum
Association of Midwestern Universities, Sept.-Oct. 1955, no.
16; Tulsa, Oklahoma, Philbrook Art Center, *Four Centuries of
European Art,* Oct. 1956, no. 34; Oklahoma City, Oklahoma,
Oklahoma Art Center, *Four Centuries of European Art,* Nov.
1957, no. 23; Little Rock, Arkansas, Museum of Fine Arts,
Dec. 1958, no. 30; Phoenix, Arizona, Phoenix Art Museum,
One Hundred Years of French Painting, 1860-1960, Feb. 1-
Feb. 26, 1961, no. 42 (lent by Count Ivan Podgoursky, San
Antonio, Texas); Oakland, California, Oakland Art Museum,
One Hundred Years of French Painting, 1860-1960, Mar. 5-
Mar. 31, 1961, no. 42; New York, Christie Manson & Woods
(U.S.A.) Ltd., *Van Gogh, Gauguin and Their Circle,* Nov.
1968, no. 9

Exhibitions: See catalog ref. page
First Exhibited: II

Literature: Charels Chassé, *Gauguin et le Groupe de Pont-
Aven,* Paris: H. Floury, 1921, pp. 48-50; *American Art
Journal,* 1923-24, vol. 20, p. 275; Jean de Rotonchamp,
Gauguin, Paris: Les Editions G. Crès et Cie,
1925, p. 70; *Canadian Art,* Summer 1949, vol. VI, no. 4, p. 176,
repr.; J. Loize, *Les Amitiés du peintre Georges-Daniel de
Monfried et ses reliques de Gauguin,* 1951, no. 108, pp. 86-87;
Charles Chassé, *Gauguin et son Temps,* 1955, pp. 70, 79;
M. Malingue, "Du Nouveau sur Gauguin," *L'Oeil,* July-Aug.
1959, p. 38; John Rewald, *Le Post-Impressionnisme,* Paris:
Albin Michel, 1961, p. 176; Georges Baudaille, *Gauguin,*
London: 1964, pp. 89, 130, repr. in color; Georges Wildenstein,
Gauguin Oeuvre Catalogue, Paris: 1964, no. 321, pp. 121-122;
Art in America, Sept. 1969, p. 15, repr.; *Art News,* Sept. 1969,
p. 26, repr.; *Apollo,* Oct. 1969, p. IX, repr.; *Connaissance
des Arts,* Oct. 1969, p. 67, repr.; *Apollo,* Feb. 1970, p. 170,
repr.; *Connoisseur,* Feb. 1970, p. 116, repr.; Frank Davis,
"A Royal Record of Portraiture," *Country Life,* Feb. 5,
1970, pp. 302-303, repr.

**In 1889 Gauguin and the painters working with him
transferred their Breton activities from Pont Aven to Le
Pouldu, which they found more primitive. In October of
that year they moved to an inn kept by Marie Henry and
soon thereafter began decorating its walls with
paintings and sculpture. Gauguin's *Bonjour Monsieur
Gauguin* occupied the upper panel of a door in the inn.
There are two existing versions of the composition, and
both Wildenstein and Sutton are agreed that the
Hammer picture is the one originally fastened to the
door at Le Pouldu while the Prague version precedes it
or is a later replica. In any case, the two pictures
cannot have been created more than a few weeks apart.
This picture is distinguished from the Prague version by
a somewhat more unified composition and more
consistent brushwork. The subject was almost certainly**

**inspired by Courbet's *Bonjour Monsieur Courbet*
which Gauguin and van Gogh had seen on a visit to
Montpellier in December 1888. A related watercolor
on silk (*Rewald, Gauguin Drawings,* no. 18) is apparently
a study for the righthand figure in the Prague version.**

34 Vincent VAN GOGH (1853-1890)

Garden of the Rectory at Nuenen, 1885
Oil on canvas, mounted on panel
20 7/8″ x 30 3/4″ (53.0 x 78.2 cm.)

Collections: Oldenzeel Gallery, Rotterdam, 1903; Jan Smit,
Alblasserdam (Sale, Amsterdam, Mak van Waiij, Feb. 10,
1919, no. 30, repr.): L. J. Smith, Kinderdijk; Leo C. Smit,
Kinderdijk, 1952; (Sale, New York, Parke-Bernet Galleries,
Inc., Nov. 20, 1968, no. 37): Spencer Samuel & Co., Ltd.,
New York: Fletcher Jones, Los Angeles

Exhibited: Rotterdam, Oldenzeel Gallery, *Van Gogh,* 1904, no.
31; The Hague, Gemeentemuseum, *Vincent van Gogh,* Mar. 30-
May 17, 1953; no. 31; Otterloo, Rijksmuseum Kröller-Müller,
Vincent van Gogh, May 24-July 19, 1953, no. 18;
Amsterdam, Stedelijk Museum, *Vincent van Gogh,* July 23-
Sept. 20, 1953, no. 18; Dordrecht, Dordrecht Museum, *Boem,
Bloem en Plant,* July 16-Aug. 31, 1955, no. 52; Paris Musée
Jacquemart-André, *Vincent van Gogh,* Feb.-March
1960, no. 11, p. 30

Exhibitions: See catalog ref. page
First Exhibited: III
Not Exhibited: XX, XXIII

Literature: *Vincent van Gogh, Brieven aan Zijn Broeder* (ed.
J. van Gogh-Bonger), Amsterdam: 1914, Letter 394, vol. II,
p. 463; *The Letters of Vincent van Gogh to his Brother,* London:
Constable & Co., Ltd., New York: Houghton Mifflin, 1927,
Letter 394, pp. 456-458; J.B. de la Faille, *L'Oeuvre de
Vincent van Gogh, Catalogue Raisonné,* Paris and Brussels:
Editions G. van Oest, 1928, vol. I. no. 67, vol. II, pl. XX
(measurements incorrect); Dr. Walter Vanbeselaere, *De
Hollandsche Periode (1880-1885) in Het Werk van Vincent
van Gogh,* Antwerp: De Sikkel, 1937, pp. 294, 352, 414; J.B.
de la Faille, *Vincent van Gogh,* Paris: Hyperion Press, 1938,
no. 73, p. 79 (measurements incorrect); J.B. de la Faille, *The
Works of Vincent van Gogh, His Paintings and Drawings,*
Amsterdam: Meulenhoff International, New York: Reynal &
Co. with William Morris & Co., Inc. 1970, no. F67, pp. 66,
614, repr. p. 67; Sale catalog, *Impressionist and Modern
Paintings and Sculptures,* London: Sotheby & Co., Apr. 15,
1970, no. 26, p. 55, repr. opp. in color

**In the late winter of 1885-86 van Gogh wrote to his
brother that, "When there was snow, I...painted a few**

studies of our garden," and de la Faille dates this picture to January 1885. The scene is taken from the presbytery at Nuenen, the small town in which van Gogh's father was vicar and where Vincent lived with his family for two years before going to France. The distant tower occurs in several pictures of the time, and there exist another painting and two drawings directly related to this scene (de la Faille 185, 1133, 1234). The picture projects the bleakness Vincent felt around him in the winter of 1885, a bleakness which permeates both his landscapes and his figure studies. It is among the last of his "Dutch" pictures, worked out in the dark tonalities of the Hague school, its drawing perhaps indebted to the English illustration he knew so well. The extreme lightness of the sky forecasts the future lightening of van Gogh's palette and suggests that interest in color to which he referred constantly in his letters of the period.

35   Vincent VAN GOGH (1853-1890)

Lilacs, 1887
Oil on canvas: 10 3/4" x 13 15/16" (27.3 x 35.3 cm.)

Collections: Drs. Fritz and Peter Nathan, Zurich

Exhibitions: See catalog ref. page
First Exhibited: IX
Not Exhibited: XXIII

Literature: J. B. de la Faille, *The Works of Vincent van Gogh, His Paintings and Drawings,* Amsterdam: Meulenhoff International, New York: Reynal & Co. with William Morrow & Co., Inc., 1970, p. 142, no. 286b

———————————

Van Gogh had been preoccupied with bringing more intense color into his pictures well before his move to Paris in 1886. It was only under the direct impact of the paintings he saw in the French capital, however, that he began to use color freely, applying it with an increasingly divisionist brushstroke. Toward the fall of 1887 Vincent wrote to the English painter Levens, "I have lacked money for paying models else I had entirely given myself to figure painting. But I have made a series of color studies in painting, simply flowers, red poppies, blue cornflowers and myosotes, white and red roses, yellow chrysanthemums—seeking oppositions of blue with orange, red and green, yellow and violet seeking *les tons rompus et neutres* to harmonize brutal extremes. Trying to render intense colour and not a grey harmony." The present picture is no doubt one of these studies.

36   Vincent VAN GOGH (1853-1890)

The Sower, 1888
Oil on canvas: 13 1/4" x 15 15/16" (33.6 x 40.4 cm.)

Collections: Mme. J. van Gogh-Bonger, Amsterdam; Montross Gallery, New York, 1921; Reverend Theodore Pitcairn, Bryn Athyn, Pennsylvania

Exhibited: New York, Montross Gallery, Oct. 1920; Philadelphia, Pennsylvania, Philadelphia Museum of Art, Summer Loan, 1960 (lent by Rev. Theodore Pitcairn)

Exhibitions: See catalog ref. page
First Exhibited: II
Not Exhibited: X, XX, XXIII

Literature: J. B. de la Faille, *The Works of Vincent van Gogh, His Paintings and Drawings,* Amsterdam: Meulenhoff International, New York: Reynal & Co. with William Morrow & Co., Inc. 1970, pp. 240, 634, no. 575a, repr. p. 240; Sale catalog, *Important Impressionist and Modern Drawings, Paintings and Sculpture,* London: Christie, Manson & Woods, May 2, 1969, p. 46, no. 58, repr. opp. p. 46

———————————

The Sower was a theme which fascinated van Gogh throughout his career, partly because of his Millet-inspired identification with the peasant subject and partly for psychologically more deep-seated associations with fertility and generation. This version of the subject is unique in placing the sower's figure against a silhouette of Arles, something van Gogh otherwise reserved for pictures of reapers or plowed fields (de la Faille 465, 545). The character of the brushwork and the nature and intensity of the color suggest a date in late 1888 or early 1889, conceivably even one as late in 1889 as van Gogh's stay at the hospital of Saint-Rémy. The size and intensity of the blue-purple field, "compulsive in its excess" (Meyer Schapiro), swallows the figure, adding to the picture's disharmonious scale relationships. These do not, however, detract from the power of this small canvas.

37   Vincent VAN GOGH (1853-1890)

Hospital at Saint-Rémy, 1889
Oil on canvas: 35 1/2" x 28" (90.2 x 71.1 cm.)

Collections: A. Schuffenecker, Paris: Galerie E. Druet, Paris, 1907; Dr. J. Keller, Paris 1908-10; Galerie E. Druet, Paris, 1910; Paul von Mendelssohn-Bartholdy, Berlin, 1911; Paul Rosenberg & Co., New York; Norton Simon, Los Angeles, 1964 (Sale, New York, Parke-Bernet Galleries, Inc. May 5, 1971, no. 48)

Exhibited: Paris, Galerie Druet, *Vincent van Gogh,* Jan. 6-18, 1908, no. 16; Berlin, Galerie Paul Cassirer, *Vincent van Gogh,* May-June 1914, no. 65; Amsterdam, Stedelijk Museum, *Vincent van Gogh en Zijn Tijdgenooten,* Sept. 6-Nov. 2, 1930, no. 92; Frankfurt, Städelsches Kunstinstitut, *Vom Abbild zum Sinnbild,* June 3-July 3, 1931, no. 69

Exhibitions: See catalog ref. page
First Exhibited: IX

Literature: Louis Piérard, *La Vie Tragique de Vincent van Gogh,* Paris: Les Editions G. Cres et Cie, 1924, p. 184, repr.; *Aesculape,* XIIIth Year, II, Nov., 1923, p. 250; Roch Grey, *Vincent van Gogh,* Rome: Editions de Valori Plastici, Imprimerie R. Garroni, repr.; *Aesculape,* XVIth Year, VI, June, 1926, p. 158; Florent Fels, *Vincent van Gogh,* Paris: H. Floury, 1928, p. 171, repr.; J. B. de la Faille, *L'Oeuvre de Vincent van Gogh, Catalogue Raisonné,* Paris and Brussels: Editions G. van Oest, 1928, no. 643, vol. II, pl. CLXXIX; Victor Doiteau and Edgar Leroy, *La Folie de van Gogh* (préface Paul Gachet), Paris: Editions Aesculape, 1928, p. 64 repr. opp.; *The Letters of Vincent van Gogh to His Brother,* Memoir by J. van Gogh-Bonger, London: Constable & Co., Ltd., Boston and New York: Houghton Mifflin Co., 1929, vol. III, Letter 610, p. 400; Stedelijk Museum catalog: *Vincent van Gogh en Zijn Trijdgenooten,* Amsterdam: H. G. van Dorssen, 1930, no. 92, p. 18, Städelsches Kunstinstitut catalog: *Austellung von Meisterwerken, Moderner Malerie, Vom Abbild zum Sinnbild,* Frankfurt: August Osterrieth, 1931, no. 69, p. 26; John Rewald, "Van Gogh en Provence," *l'Amour de l'Art,* VIII, Oct., 1936, Paris: Editions A. Sedrowski, p. 297, repr.; W. Scherjon and W. Jos. de Gruyter, *Vincent van Gogh's Great Period,* Amsterdam: "De Spieghel," Ltd., 1937, p. 205, repr.; J. B. de la Faille, *Vincent van Gogh* (preface Charles Terrasse), Paris, London, and New York: Editions Hyperion, 1939, no. 648, p. 446, repr.; Dr. François-Joachim Beer, *Du Démon de Van Gogh,* (after *Van Gogh à l'Asile,* by Dr. Edgar Leroy) Nice: Imprimerie Nouvelles Réunis, 1945, p. 75; J. B. de la Faille, *The Works of Vincent Van Gogh, His Paintings and Drawings,* Amsterdam: Meulenhoff International, New York: Reynal & Co. with William Morrow & Co., 1970, no. F643, pp. 256, 636, repr. p.257; Sale catalog, *Highly Important 19th and 20th Century Paintings, Drawings, and Sculpture, from the Private Collection of Norton Simon,* New York: Parke-Bernet Galleries, Inc., May 5, 1971, no. 48, p. 92, repr. in color

---

Van Gogh stayed at the hospital at Saint-Rémy for almost exactly one year, from May 1889 until May 1890, and took its gardens and surroundings as the subject for many of his pictures. In the fall of 1889 he wrote to his brother Theo that he had "two views of the park and the asylum," one of which was undoubtedly this work. Only one other painting (de la Faille 653) shows a substantial portion of the facade of the hospital. One sees in this picture the remnants of an older style in the squared rendering of the building, while the flame-like brushwork of the trees, which Vincent saw as "warped as in old wood," announces the style for which he has become best known. Few of van Gogh's pictures show as well as this the tendency of his brushstrokes to cling to the surface of the canvas or the increasing density and intensity of his paint application during the last three years of his life.

38 Henri de TOULOUSE-LAUTREC (1864-1901)

In the Salon, 1894
Oil on cardboard, 15 3/4″ x 23 7/8″ (40.0 x 60.6 cm.)
Signed lower left: H.-T. Lautrec

Collections: Octave Maus, Brussels (acquired from the artist about 1896); Tetze-Lund, Copenhagen; J. K. Thannhauser, New York; Paul Rosenberg, New York; Sale, London, Sotheby & Co., Nov. 7, 1962, no. 85, repr. in color; Galerie Beyeler, Basel; Hammer Galleries, New York

Exhibited: Paris Galerie Manzi et Joyant, *Toulouse-Lautrec,* 1896; Brussels, *Exposition Toulouse-Lautrec,* organized by La Libre Esthétique, Mar. 1902; Paris, Galerie Manzi et Joyant, *Exposition Retrospective de L'Oeuvre de H. Toulouse-Lautrec,* June 15-July 11, 1914, no. 39

Exhibitions: See catalog ref. page
First Exhibited: I
Not Exhibited: XX, XXIII, XXXI, XXXII, XXXIII

Literature: Maurice Joyant, *Henri de Toulouse-Lautrec,* Paris: H. Floury, 1926, p. 286; Gotthard Jedlicka, *Henri de Toulouse-Lautrec,* Erienbach-Zurich: E. Rentsch, 1943; p. 321, repr. opp. p. 218; Francis Jourdin Jean Adhémar, *Toulouse-Lautrec,* Paris: P. Tisné, 1952, repr. pl. 84; Sale catalog, *Impressionist and Modern Paintings, Drawings and Sculpture,* London, Sotheby & Co., Nov. 7, 1962, no. 85, repr. in color; P. Huisman and M. G. Dortu, *Lautrec by Lautrec,* New York: Viking Press, 1964, pp. 130-131, repr. in color; *Apollo,* Sept. 1966, p. LXXV, repr.; "On the Market," *Apollo,* Nov. 1968, p. 395, repr.; Francois Daulte, "Hammer en dix chefs-d'oeuvre," *Connaissance des Arts,* Sept. 1970, p. 79, repr.; *Connoisseur,* Nov. 1970, p. 210, repr.

From 1892 until 1895 Toulouse-Lautrec produced a series of pictures of prostitutes and bordello scenes. The summation of this work was the large canvas, *Au salon de la rue des Moulins,* painted in 1894 and now in the museum at Albi. There is a pastel version of the complete composition in the same museum and a large group of related studies of which this picture is one. Presumably also executed in 1894, it represents the same two women who are seated at the left rear center of the Albi painting. According to Joyant, the woman seen in profile is the Rolande of several of the other studies.

In transferring the figures to the larger work Lautrec has altered only the position of the arms. The technique of this study is much broader than that of the finished picture, and its color is worked out in terms of close-valued, close-hued, and astringent contrasts in Lautrec's most expressive manner. Octave Maus is said to have acquired this picture in 1896, perhaps directly from the Manzi-Joyant exhibition at which the bordello scenes were shown by Lautrec in two small locked rooms.

39 Pierre BONNARD (1867-1947)

Street Scene, ca. 1902
Oil on canvas: 21″ x 27 1/2″ (53.3 x 69.8 cm.)
Signed lower right: Bonnard

Collections: Viscount Jowitt, London; Noel Coward, London; Sale, London Sotheby & Co., Apr. 18, 1956, no. 14, repr; Schoneman Galleries, New York; Sale, London, Christie, Manson & Woods, Dec. 1, 1967, p. 34, no. 37, repr.

Exhibited: Scotland, Edinburgh Festival, *Bonnard and Vuillard,* Aug. 1948, no. 55 (repr. p. 7); London, Roland, Browse and Delbanco, *Bonnard,* 1950, no. 16 (repr.); London, Redfern Gallery, *French Paintings,* Oct. 30-Nov. 22, 1952, no. 53

Exhibitions: See catalog ref. page
First Exhibited: I
Not Exhibited: XXIII

Literature: Sale catalog, London: Sotheby & Co., Apr. 18, 1956, no. 144, repr.; *L'Oeil,* no. 21, Sept. 1956, p. 44; Denys Sutton, intro., *Bonnard,* London: Farber Gallery, 1957, p. 12, repr. in color pl. 5; Jean and Henry Dauberville, *Bonnard, Catalogue Raisonné, de l'Oeuvre Peint,* 1888-1905, Paris: Bernheim-Jeune, 1965, vol. I, p. 26, no. 269, repr.; Sale catalog, *Important Impressionist and Modern Drawings, Paintings and Sculpture,* London: Christie, Manson & Woods, Dec. 1, 1967, p. 34, no. 37, repr. in color

———————————

Although the relatively muted tones, small-scale paint application, and areas of bare canvas in this picture recall the early style Bonnard shared with Vuillard, one already senses the richness of his later color in the red-blue contrasts. The tree trunks hold the composition firmly in place, making it almost a triptych, a favorite Nabi format.

40 Pierre BONNARD (1867-1947)

Nude against the Light, 1909
Oil on canvas: 48 3/4″ x 21 1/2″ (123.8 x 54.6 cm.)
Signed lower left: Bonnard

Collections: Galerie Bernheim-Jeune (acquired from the artist Jan. 8, 1909); Henri Bernstein, Paris, Jan. 8, 1910 (Sale, Paris, June 9, 1911); Repurchased by Bernheim-Jeune; Emile Maysisch, Paris; Marianne Feilchenfeldt, Zurich; Ragnar Moltzau, Oslo; Michel P. Couturier, Neuilly-sur-Seine; Adler Collection, London (Sale, New York, Parke-Bernet Galleries, Inc., Mar. 21, 1962, no. 80, repr.); Galerie der Spiegel, Cologne; Alex Léfèvre Gallery, London; Norton Simon (Sale, New York, Parke-Bernet Galleries, Inc., May 5, 1971, no. 59, repr.)

Exhibited: Zurich, Kunsthaus, *Bonnard,* 1949; Copenhagen, Ny Carlsberg Glyptotek, *Fra Renoir til Villon, Franske Malerier eg. Udlaant fra Ragnar Moltzau Samling,* June 21-Aug. 1, 1956 (hors cat.) and the Hague, Gemeentemuseum, Collection Moltzau, Apr.-June 1957, no. 15; Scotland, Edinburgh Festival, and London, Tate Gallery, *Bonnard,* 1958, no. 13; Exposition organized by the Arts Council of Edinburgh and London, *Documenta III,* 1958, no. 13; Copenhagen, Ny Carlsberg, Glyptotek, 1959; Paris, Galerie Europe, *Itinéraire sur Trois Générations,* June-July 1960, no. 4; London, Léfevre Gallery, *XIXth and XXth Century French Paintings,* Oct. 14-Nov. 13, 1965, no. 1

Exhibitions: See catalog ref. page
First Exhibited: IX, XXIII

Literature: Gustave Coquiot, *Bonnard,* Paris: Editions Bernheim-Jeune, 1922, pl. 5, repr.; *Art and Auctions,* vol. 6, no. 121, Feb. 28, 1962, pp. 29, 35; Sale catalog, *Important Modern Paintings, Drawings, Bronzes,* New York: Parke-Bernet Galleries, Inc., Mar. 21, 1962, no. 80 repr.; *Arts,* Mar. 1962, repr. p. 13; *Apollo,* Oct. 1965, repr. p. 338; J. and H. Dauberville, *Bonnard, Catalogue Raisonné,* Paris: Editions Bernheim-Jeune, 1968, vol. II, no. 528, repr. p. 140; Sale catalog, *Highly Important 19th and 20th Century Paintings, Drawings & Sculpture, from the Private Collection of Norton Simon,* New York: Parke-Bernet Galleries, Inc., May 5, 1971, no. 59, p. 114, repr. in color

———————————

Strongest as a colorist, weakest as a draftsman, Bonnard was often at his best when a canvas of strongly marked shape helped him structure his composition. In this picture the rectangular shapes at the top and left side assist in giving firmness, as do the value contrasts caused by the backlighting of the figure. For the rest, Bonnard is free to indulge the lavish richness of his purples, golds, and dark greens. Consistently attracted to the timeless theme of the bather, he has here used a languid pose recalling that of the traditional, *La Source.* The picture was said by Coquiot to date from 1908, although the Daubervilles assign it to 1909.

41 Emile BERNARD (1868-1941)

Wheat Harvest
Oil on canvas: 28 1/2″ x 35 7/8″ (72.4 x 91.1 cm.)
Signed and dated lower left: Bernard 1889

Collections: Clement Altarriba (son-in-law of the artist),
Paris; Wildenstein & Co., Inc., New York; Mr. and Mrs.
Richard Sussman, New York; Findlay Galleries, Inc.,
Chicago

Exhibitions: See catalog ref. page
First Exhibited: II
Not Exhibited: XX, XXIII

Literature: John Rewald, *Post Impressionism,* New York:
Museum of Modern Art, 1956, repr. p. 285; *Connoisseur,*
Nov. 1966, repr. p. XCIII; *Art Journal,* Winter 1966-1967,
repr. p. 195

———————

**The harvesting of wheat was among the favorite themes
of the group gathered around Gauguin in Brittany
during the years 1889-1890. Bernard had treated the
subject in painting in 1888 and in a print in 1889, the
year of this picture, and Gauguin had also painted
Breton haymakers in 1889 (cf. his *Breton Landscape*
in the de Sylva Collection of the Los Angeles County
Museum of Art). Bernard, forbidden by his father to join
Gauguin at Pont-Aven, passed the summer of 1889 at
Saint-Briac where this picture was probably painted. One
sees in the flat color areas reminiscences of the Japanese
prints so popular with the Pont-Aven group, and in the
outlining of the shapes the "cloisonnism" identified
in their work by Edouard Dujardin. At this particular
moment Bernard had carried flatness and clear
separation of colors considerably further than Gauguin,
although his facture (and Gauguin's of the period) recalls
Cézanne's version of the Impressionist comma-like
brushwork with its groups of parallel strokes. In the
cross on the distant hill one can perhaps see a forecast
of the mystical Catholicism that was increasingly to
occupy Bernard.**

42 Edouard VUILLARD (1868-1940)

In the Bus, ca. 1895
Oil on board: 9 13/16″ x 9″ (25.0 x 22.9 cm.)
Signed lower right: E. Vuillard

Collections: Geroges Seligmann, New York; Dalzell Hatfield
Galleries, Los Angeles; Stephen Hahn Gallery, New York

Exhibitions: See catalog ref. page

First Exhibited: I
Not Exhibited: XX, XXIII

———————

**The *tachiste* paint application, which results in an
allover decorative pattern, and the predominance of
low-keyed golden browns are characteristic of Vuillard
at this date. The subject of the painting is by no means
clear.**

43 Edouard VUILLARD (1868-1940)

At the Seashore, ca. 1904
Oil on panel: 8 1/2″ x 8 1/2″ (21.6 x 21.6 cm.)
Signed lower left: E. Vuillard

Collections: Joseph Hessel, Paris; Alfred Daber, Paris; Sam
Salz, New York; Mr. and Mrs. Henry R. Luce, New York

Exhibited: Paris, Musée du Louvre, Pavillon Marsan, *Vuillard,*
1938; Paris, Galerie Charpentier, *Vuillard,* 1946; New York,
Museum of Modern Art, and Cleveland Museum of Art,
Edouard Vuillard, 1954 (cat. p. 103)

Exhibitions: See catalog ref. page
First Exhibited: II
Not Exhibited: XI, XXIII
Exhibited: Toronto, Ontario, Art Gallery of Ontario, *Edouard
Vuillard,* Sept. 11-Oct. 24, 1971, and San Francisco, California,
Palace of the Legion of Honor, Nov. 18, 1971-Jan. 2, 1972;
Chicago, Illinois, Art Institute of Chicago, *Edouard Vuillard,*
Jan. 28-Mar. 12, 1972, no. 59

Literature: Jacques Salomon, *Vuillard,* Paris: Gallimard, 1968,
no. 100, as *Lucie Hessel devant la Mer,* repr. in color;
François Daulte, "Hammer en dix chefs-d'oeuvre,"
Connaissance des Arts, no. 233, Sept. 1970, p. 85, repr. in
color; John Russell, *Edouard Vuillard* (exhibition cat.),
Toronto: Art Gallery of Ontario, 1971, p. 231, repr. pl. 59

———————

**"This little painting," wrote Jacques Salomon, "is like
a cry from the heart, the echo of which ravished me when
I admired it on Lucie Hessel's mantelpiece; the touch
is so alive, so alert, so completely submissive to the
rhythm of Vuillard's feeling." Vuillard first met
Mme. Hessel in 1900, and it was in her apartment in
the Rue de Rivoli that he henceforth found most of his
sitters, the most constant of these being Mme. Hessel
herself. She was, in Jacques Salomon's words, "beautiful
and elegant, without being pretty. Mme. Hessel joined
great qualities of judgment and feeling to a real
distinction. Vuillard devoted to her a constant friendship
which for forty years was not troubled by the slightest
cloud." Lucie Hessel was the wife of Joseph Hessel,**

first director of the Galerie Bernheim-Jeune and later an important independent dealer in Rue La Böetie.

44 Edouard VUILLARD (1868-1940)
Rue Lepic, Paris, 1908
Tempera: 65″ x 18 1/2″ (165.1 x 47.0 cm.)
Signed lower right: E. Vuillard

Collections: Sam Salz, New York; Mr. and Mrs. Henry R. Luce, New York

Exhibitions: See catalog ref. page
First Exhibited: II
Not Exhibited: XXI, XXII, XXIII, XXIV, XXV, XXVI, XXVII, XXVIII, XXIX, XXX, XXXI, XXXII, XXXIII

Literature: Claude Roger-Marx, *Vuillard et son Temps,* Paris: Arts et Métiers Graphiques, 1945, p. 140 (original projects, with additional twelve inches of sky, reproduced p. 161); John Russell, *Edouard Vuillard* (exhibition ct.), Toronto: Art Gallery of Toronto, 1971, p. 232, no. 69, repr. pl. 69

———————————

The tall, narrow format imposed by projects for decorative screens or room panels seem to have been particularly congenial to the Nabis. In this one the matte paint application, leaving space for the support to show through, may evidence Vuillard's awareness to Toulouse-Lautrec. The composition, cut down by about a foot from its original dimensions, was one of a series of sketches of streets and squares of Paris for a projected room decoration for Henri Bernstein. Roger-Marx reproduces it in its original size next to a similar panel of a park in Paris. The Rue Lepic runs into the Place Blanche in Montmartre, the center of Nabi activity.

45 Edouard VUILLARD (1868-1940)

Interior, ca. 1910
Oil on board: 21 1/8″ x 15 7/8″ (53.3 x 40.3 cm.)
Stamped lower right: E. Vuillard (see Lugt 2497a)*

Collections: The Hanover Gallery, London; Edward Le Bas, Brighton (Sale, Geneva, Christie, Manson & Woods, Nov. 6, 1969, no. 164, repr.)

Exhibited: London, Royal Academy of Arts, *A Painter's Collection* (Edward Le Bas Coll.), Mar. 19-Apr. 28, 1963, no. 120

Exhibitions: See catalog ref. page
First Exhibited: III
Not Exhibited: XXIII

Literature: Sale catalog: *Impressionist and Modern Drawings, Paintings and Sculpture,* Geneva: Christie, Manson & Woods, Nov. 6, 1969, no. 164, repr.

———————————

Lighter in tone than is common for Vuillard, this airy composition is held together by the rectangular forms of the window, doorway, and chair, and by the strong vertical of the open door. Interiors without figures are rare for Vuillard. In this case, the scene may be that of his studio on the Boulevard Malsherbes.

*See Frits Lugt, *Les Marques de Collections, de Dessins & d'Estampes,* Le Haye 1956, Supplement, pp. 363-364. After Vuillard's death his sister and brother-in-law, M. & Mme. K-X Roussel, put stamps (E Vuillard or E V) on the works which remained in his studio as well as on a few which belonged to the family or to Vuillard's close friends.

46 Georges ROUAULT (1871-1958)

Circus Girl, 1939
Oil on paper 25 3/4″ x 20 11/16″ (65.4 x 52.5 cm.)
Signed lower right: G. Rouault

Collections: Ambroise Vollard, Paris; Edwin C. Vogel, New York; Perls Gallery, New York; Vladimir Golschmann, St. Louis; Stephen Hahn Gallery, New York

Exhibited: London, C.E.M.A. Exhibition, *20th Century French Paintings and Drawings,* 1943, no. 10; London, Royal Academy of Arts, *A Painter's Collection,* (Edward Le Bas Coll.), Mar. 19-Apr. 28, 1963, no. 10

Exhibitions: See catalog ref. page
First Exhibited: I
Not Exhibited: X, XX, XXIII

———————————

It is possible to see in Rouault's heavily-impastoed and stained-glass-like style a reflection of the bejeweled richness of the style of his master, Gustave Moreau. Both Rouault's style and his subjects, of which the circus was one, altered little throughout his career. In 1938, approximately the date of this picture, he completed a series of seven etchings and eighty-two wood engravings for André Sauarès' *Le Cirque.* There are at least four other pictures with the same subject and title as this (Courthion 305, 307, 310, Glasgow).

47 Maurice de VLAMINCK (1876-1958)

Summer Bouquet
Oil on canvas: 25 3/4″ x 21 9/16″ (65.4 x 54.7 cm.)
Signed lower left: Vlaminck

Collections: James Vigeveno Galleries, Los Angeles;
Mr. and Mrs. Henry R. Luce, New York

Exhibitions: See catalog ref. page
First Exhibited: IV
Not Exhibited: XX, XXIII

_____

Vlaminck was so prolific as a landscape painter that
his vases of flowers are comparatively rare. Yet he did,
however, paint flower still lifes sporadically through
most of his career. Of this rather late work, John Walker
wrote in a manuscript note on the Hammer Collection:
"His handling of the thick, juicy paint which is one of his
most attractive talents is here beautifully displayed,
especially in the petals of the flowers. De Stael never
produced a more brilliant display of palette-knife
virtuosity."

48 André DERAIN (1880-1954)

Still Life with Basket, Jug and Fruit, 1911
Oil on canvas: 19 7/8" x 23 11/16" (50.5 x 60.1 cm.)
Signed lower right: a derain

Collections: Galerie Simon, Paris; Galerie Matthieson, Berlin;
Edward Le Bas, Brighton

Exhibited: New York, Galerie Chalette, 1958; Tokyo, National
Museum of Art, Oct. 1-Nov. 10, 1963; Kyoto, National Art
Gallery of Kyoto, Nov. 20-Dec. 10, 1963

Exhibitions: See catalog ref. page
First Exhibited: III
Not Exhibited: XX, XXIII

Literature: *L'Esprit Nouveau*, May 1921, repr.; Sale catalog,
Impressionist and Modern Drawings, Paintings and Sculpture,
Geneva: Christie, Manson & Woods, Nov. 6, 1969, no. 165, repr.

_____

At the same that he was painting more clearly
Cubist-derived works, Derain was also working in the
flatter, heavier style of this picture. One sees the
influence of Cubism in the stylization of the shapes, the
paint application of the background, and the restricted
palette. The particular range of dark hues employed in
this picture was favored by Derain throughout his career,
and the style of this work is in every way more prophetic
of his future than were many of the paintings executed
at this time.

49 Amedeo MODIGLIANI (1884-1920)

Woman of the People, 1918
Oil on canvas: 39 1/4" x 25 3/8" (99.7 x 65. 1 cm.)
Signed upper right: Modigliani

Collections: André Léfèvre, Paris; Blair Laing, Toronto,
Canada; Dr. Armand Hammer, Los Angeles; Los Angeles
County Museum of Art (Gift of Dr. and Mrs. Armand
Hammer, 1968)

Exhibited: Brussels, Palais des Beaux-Arts, *Modigliani*, 1933,
no 53; Paris, Petit Palais, *Les Maîtres de l'Art Indépendants,
1895-1937*, June-Oct. 1937, no. 77; Paris, Musée National
d'Art Moderne, *L'Oeuvre du XXème Siècle*, May-June 1952,
no. 73; London, The Arts Council, *XXth Century
Masterpieces*, 1952, no. 67; Paris, Musée National d'Art
Moderne, *Collection André Léfèvre*, Mar.-Apr. 1964, no. 209

Exhibitions: See catalog ref. page
First Exhibited: I
Not Exhibited: IV, VI, VII, IX, XXI, XXII, XXIII

Literature: Maurice Raynal *Peintres du XXème Siècle*,
Geneva: 1947, repr. in color pl. 38; Maurice Raynal, *La
Peinture Française Contemporaine*, Geneva: Skira, ca. 1960,
repr. in color pl. 37 and on cover; *Modigliani*, New York:
Skira Color Prints, n.d., pl. I; Claude Roy, *Modigliani*,
Geneva: Skira, 1958 (The Taste of Our Time), p. 80, repr.;
Sale catalog, *Vente Léfèvre*, Paris: Palais Galliera, Nov. 25,
1965, repr.

_____

This portrait of Germaine Lable, daughter of the
concierge of the artist's close friend, the poet Max
Jacob, was painted in 1918, two years before
Modigliani's premature death at the age of thirty-six.

The painting exemplifies Modigliani's distinctive
ability to capture the unique characterization of his
sitter through, or one might almost say despite, his
personal, elegantly mannered style of portraiture. The
elongated oval face, drooping shoulder lines and pursed
lips were all favorite devices of the artist. The delicately
balanced facial features and the graceful curves of
hairline, scarf, and drapery reveal the artist's masterful
draftsmanship.

This commonplace woman of the people, seated in a
basically static frontal position, is juxtaposed to the
diagonal angle of the bed so that the curvilinear pattern
of the head rail and pillow complement the curves in
the figure and create a dynamic interplay of
compositional forces. The combination of spatial flatness
and subtle distortions of linear and shape relationships
results in a unified, highly evocative composition;
the abstract rhythm of formal elements across the
pictorial surface alone carries the weight of the personal
content. It is precisely this way of conveying incisive
characterization with the most elegant and sparse formal
means that makes Modigliani so moving and original
an artist.

50 Marie LAURENCIN (1885-1956)

Women in the Forest
Oil on canvas: 33 7/8" x 39 5/8" (81.0 x 100.7 cm.)
Signed and dated lower right: Marie Laurencin 1920

Collections: Paul Rosenberg, Paris; John Quinn, New York;
Forrestal, New York; Martin Horrell, New York; Leo Aarons,
New York; Stephen Hahn Gallery, New York

Exhibited: New York, Art Center, *Memorial Exhibition of the
John Quinn Collection,* Jan. 8-30, 1926

Exhibitions: See catalog ref. page
First Exhibited: II
Not Exhibited: X, XX, XXIII

Literature: Roger Allard, *Marie Laurencin* (Les Peintres
Français Nouveaux, no. 9), Paris: Gallimard, 1921, repr. p.
49; Forbes Watson, *John Quinn 1870-1925, Collection of
Paintings, Water Colors, Drawings & Sculpture,* Huntington,
New York: Pidgeon Hill Press, 1926, p. 11, repr. p. 66; B. L.
Reid, *The Man from New York,* New York: 1968, pp. 470-471

**Marie Laurencin was closely associated with the Cubists
before World War I and with the artists who formed
Cubist splinter movements after the War, but her style
was little affected by any of them. Guillaume Apollinaire
characterized her painting in *The Cubist Painters:*
"Like the dance, it is an infinitely gracious and
rhythmical art of enumeration." Her iconography of
sylph-like girls and gentle animals in an Arcadian
landscape is a personal lyric invention—suggestive
rather than literal. This large work, *Women in the
Forest,* seems to be a monumental restatement of
elements Laurencin had used in numerous small
paintings between 1917 and 1920.**

51 Marc CHAGALL (1887-0000)

Blue Angel
Gouache and pastel: 20" x 26" (50.8 x 66.1 cm.)

Collections: Frank Crowninshield, New York; Mr. and Mrs.
Henry R. Luce, New York

Exhibited: New York, Galerie Chalette, 1958; Tokyo,
National Museum of Art, Oct. 1-Nov. 10, 1963; Kyoto,
National Art Gallery of Kyoto, Nov. 20-Dec. 10, 1963

Exhibitions: See catalog ref. page
First Exhibited: II
Not Exhibited: X, XX, XXIII

Literature: Franz Meyer, *Marc Chagall, Life and Work,* New
York: Harry N. Abrams, Inc., 1964, no. 672, repr. p. 757

**The theatrical blue-red color harmony of this work and
its juxtaposition of normally unrelated figures, floating
and dream-like, are typical of Chagall. Although the
angel may have been particularly in Chagall's mind
because of the illustrations for the Bible he had been
commissioned by Vollard to do in the early 1920's, both
it and the bouquet of flowers are common in his scenes
of lovers and newlyweds. Franz Meyer suggests that the
"new natural sensuousness" of the pictures of 1937-1939
was the result of the increased security in Chagall's
personal affairs during that time.**

52 Chaim SOUTINE (1894-1943)

The Valet, 1929
Oil on canvas: 43 1/4" x 25" (109.85 x 63.0 cm.)
Signed upper right: Soutine

Collections: Pierre Loeb; Marcel Fleischmann, Zurich; Leigh B.
Block, Chicago; Paul Rosenberg, New York

Exhibitions: Not previously exhibited

53 Gilbert STUART (1755-1828)

Portrait of George Washington, 1822
Oil on canvas: 44 1/8" x 34 1/2" (112.0 x 87.6 cm.)

Collections: William D. Lewis, Philadelphia: Estate of
William D. Lewis (on loan to Pennsylvania Academy of the
Fine Arts, Philadelphia, 1881-1928); Howard Young Galleries,
New York; Mr. and Mrs. Alfred G. Wilson, Detroit (Sale,
New York: Parke-Bernet Galleries, Inc., Dec. 10, 1970, no. 12)

Exhibited: Detroit, Michigan, The Detroit Institute of Arts,
*The Eleventh Loan Exhibition, American Colonial and Early
Federal Art,* Feb. 4-Mar. 2, 1930, No. 81; Idem, *Masterpieces of
Painting from Detroit Private Collections,* Apr. 23-May 22,
1949, no. 30 (lent by Mr. and Mrs. Alfred G. Wilson in 1930
and 1949)

Exhibitions: See catalog ref. page
First Exhibited: VII
Not Exhibited: X, XX, XXIII, XXVIII, XXIX

Exhibited: Los Angeles, Los Angeles County Mueum of Art,
on exhibition, *American Paintings,* Aug. 6-Dec. 9, 1974; "Two
Hundred Years of American Painting", Traveling Exhibition,
Loan period: June 1, 1976-Jan. 15, 1977; Loan sites: Bonn,
Rheinisches Landesmuseum - Belgrade, Museum of Modern
Art - Rome, Galleria D'Arte Moderna e Contemporanea -
Warsaw, National Museum of Poland

Literature: Henry T. Tuckerman, *Book of Artists,* New York: G. P. Putnam & Son, 1867, p. 120; George C. Mason, *Life and Works of Gilbert Stuart,* New York: Charles Scribner's Sons, 1879, p. 113; Elizabeth Bryant Johnston, *Original Portraits of Washington,* Boston; James R. Osgood & Co., 1882, pp. 81, 82; Mantle Fielding, *Gilbert Stuart's Portraits of Washington,* Philadelphia: 1923, no. 30, p. 148; Lawrence Park, *Gilbert Stuart, An Illustrated Descriptive List of His Works,* New York; William Edwin Rudge, 1926, vol. II, no. 31, p. 862, John Hill Morgan and Mantle Fielding, *The Life Portraits of Washington and Their Replicas,* Philadelphia: Lancaster Press, Inc., 1931, no. 31, p. 271; G. A. Eisen, *Portraits of Washington,* New York: Robert Hamilton & Associates, 1932, p. 126, repr. p. 255; Sale catalog, *Important American Paintings, Sculpture and Drawings,* New York: Parke-Bernet Galleries, Inc., Dec. 10, 1970, no. 12, p. 14, repr. in color

Whatever Stuart's reasons for leaving Ireland in 1793, he returned to this country expecting to capitalize on the demand for portraits of George Washington. It was an astute and logical move for one of the greatest portrait painters of the period. Such was the stature of Washington, already the personification of the nation, that Stuart and his competitors, the Peales, found it profitable to devote a great part of their energy and time to recording his image.

Sittings in 1795 resulted in the "Vaughan" type of bust portrait, and in 1796 the President sat for the famous "Athenaeum" portrait now in the Boston Museum. When Senator William Bingham asked for a full-length portrait in 1796, the "Athenaeum" portrait was used as the model for the head in the composition which became known as the "Lansdowne" type. The present half-length, painted for William D. Lewis in 1822, is based on the "Lansdowne" full-length, specifically on the later version now in the New York Public Library (Lenox Collection) painted at the request of Peter Jay Munro. The basic composition is that of the Constable-Hamilton half-length of 1797, also in the New York Public Library.

54 William Michael HARNETT (1848-1892)

Still Life, 1885
Oil on panel: 13 3/4″ x 10 5/16″ (34.9 x 26.2 cm.)
Signed and dated lower left: WM Harnett 1885

Collections: George Richmond, London (Studio Sale, Christie, Manson & Woods, May 1, 1897, no. 4); Lord Justice William Rann Kennedy (Sale, London, Christie, Manson & Woods, Feb. 19, 1971, no. 177)

Exhibited: London, Royal Academy of Arts, May 1885, no. 860 (purchased by George Richmond); St. Helens, Victoria Park, *First Summer Exhibition,* 1892, no. 105

Exhibitions: See catalog ref. page
First Exhibited: IX
Not Exhibited: XX

Exhibited: Los Angeles, Los Angeles County Museum of Art, on exhibition, *American Paintings,* Aug. 6-Dec. 9, 1974

Literature: Algernon Graves, *The Royal Academy of Arts, A Complete Dictionary of Contributors and Their Work from Its Foundation in 1769 to 1904,* London: Henry Graves & Co., Ltd., and George Bell & Sons, 1905, no. 860, p. 395; *Magazine of Art,* Feb. 1951, p. 66; Alfred Frankenstein, *After the Hunt, William Harnett and Other American Still Life Painters,* Berkeley and Los Angeles: University of California Press, 1953, pp. 70-71, and rev. ed., 1969, pp. 70, 71; Sale catalog, *Pictures, Drawings, Bronzes and Prints of American, Australian, Canadian, New Zealand and South African Interest,* London: Christie, Manson & Woods, Feb. 19, 1971, no. 177, p. 49, repr. opp. in color

Though Harnett's *trompe-l'oeil* painting has a counterpart in the history of European art, it stands as a culmination of the long tradition of American Realism. Five years abroad had an effect on Harnett's work but did not erase the unique, personal elements of his style nor the stamp of forthright vision which characterizes so much of American painting.

Painted in Paris in 1885, this *Still Life* was sent to the Royal Academy in London where it was noted in the *Time* as ". . . one of the most miraculous representations . . . that we have ever seen." The writer undoubtedly was referring to the degree of realism of the painting. For, while the arrangement of solid objects in Harnett's *Still Life* does not permit the kind of visual deception typical of the more two-dimensional rack paintings in which flat objects such as cards and envelopes are mounted on a board, it nevertheless achieves an almost tangible extension into space. But Harnett achieves more than an illusion of three-dimensionality. In this work Harnett displays his particular genius in the highly sophisticated balance of color, form, and texture. Even the subtle shifts in hue among the various faded sheets of music are exploited to the fullest, and the qualities of paper, metal, leather, velvet, and wood are explored and juxtaposed so as to play the full visual scale.

Another almost identical painting at Yale University has been mistaken for this one which was bought by George Richmond from the Royal Academy in 1885. The only obvious difference between the two, probably introduced to avoid exactly the kind of problem which has arisen, is the reversal of the printed word fragments on the roll of music protruding at the left and again on the top sheet of music at the front edge of the cabinet. Apparently Harnett himself was a victim of this confusion, for, on the back of a photograph—owned by

Alfred Frankenstein—of the Yale painting, an inscription in the artist's own hand identifies it as the George Richmond still life.

55   Thomas EAKINS (1844-1916)

Portrait of Sebastiano Cardinal Martinelli, 1902
Oil on canvas, mounted on panel:
78 5/16″ x 59 15/16″ (198.9 x 152.3 cm.)
Signed lower right: Eakins 1902

Inscribed on verso: EFFIGIES SEBASTIANI S R E CARDINALIS MARTINELLI QVI ANNOS VI IN STAT FOED AB MDCCCXCVI AD MCMII DELEGATI APOSTOLICI OFFICIO FVNTVS; below: THOS. EAKINS PHILADELPHIEN A.D. MCMII PINXIT (Presently covered by panel)

Collection: The Catholic University of America, Washington, D.C. (presented by the artist in 1903) (Sale, New York, Parke-Bernet Galleries, Inc., May 21, 1970, no. 57, repr.)

Exhibited: Pittsburgh, Pennsylvania, Museum of Art, Carnegie Institute, *International Exhibition,* 1903;* Philadelphia, Pennsylvania, Pennsylvania Academy of the Fine Arts, *Thomas Eakins Memorial Exhibition,* Dec. 23, 1917-Jan. 23, 1918, no. 20; Baltimore, Maryland, Baltimore Museum of Art, *Thomas Eakins, A Retrospective Exhibition of His Paintings,* Dec. 1, 1936-Jan. 1, 1937, no. 34; Philadelphia, Pennsylvania, Philadelphia Museum of Art, *Thomas Eakins Centennial Exhibition,* 1944, no. 99; Pittsburgh, Pennsylvania, Museum of Art, Carnegie Institute, *Thomas Eakins Centennial Exhibition,* Apr. 26-June 1, 1945, no. 15, repr.; Washington, D.C., National Gallery of Art, 1969-1970; Overbrook, Pennsylvania, St. Charles Seminary, *Eakins Portraits,* 1970

Exhibitions: See catalog ref. page
First Exhibited: IV
Not Exhibited: VI, XX
Exhibited: New York, Whitney Museum of American Art, *Thomas Eakins Retrospective Exhibition,* Sept. 21-Nov. 29, 1970; Los Angeles County Museum of Art, on exhibition, *American Paintings,* Aug. 6-Dec. 9, 1974

Literature: Lloyd Goodrich, *Thomas Eakins—His Life and Work,* New York: MacMillan Co., 1933, no. 361, pp. 105-106, 194; Fairfield Porter, *Thomas Eakins,* New York: George Braziller, Inc., 1959, repr. fig. 64; Sylvan Schendler, *Thomas Eakins,* Boston; Little, Brown & Co., 1967, pp. 201, 208, 215, 296, pl. 102; Sale catalog, *18th, 19th and 20th Century American Paintings,* New York: Parke-Bernet Galleries, Inc., May 21, 1970, no. 57, p. 58, repr. opp. in color

---

As Lloyd Goodrich has pointed out, it seems paradoxical that Thomas Eakins, a Quaker and an uncompromising realist, should have begun in his late years a series of portraits of Catholic prelates. Seen as portraits of friends painted at the artist's own request, however, they begin to take their place very logically within his total oeuvre. Rejected as an artist and rather withdrawn from society, Eakins must have felt a close kinship with these learned men whose mission set them apart from the world.

In the portrait of Cardinal Martinelli, Eakins has achieved a perfect balance between the human quality of the individual and the austerity of holy office. As is often the case in Eakins' full-length portraits, this figure is placed at some distance from the viewer within a very real space, and the ambience eloquently conveys a feeling of solitary contemplation. This effect is further enhanced by the use of the profile view which presents the figure as a hieratic image to be beheld without direct involvement of the spectator. From the casually rubbed earth color suggesting wood paneling and parquet floor, to the subtle design of the rug, more or less monochromatic surroundings act as a foil, intensifying the impact of the Cardinal's presence.

*On September 16, 1903, Eakins wrote from 1729 Mt. Vernon Street, Philadelphia, to the Rector of The Catholic University of America:

Dear Sir:

I am the person who painted and presented to the University the full length portrait of Cardinal Martinelli.

I am solicited by the Carnegie Institute to exhibit specimens of my best work, and I should like to send there the Cardinal which has been exhibited in New York, Philadelphia and Chicago.

As the Carnegie Institute of Pittsburgh is absolutely fireproof I have no fear.

It will be boxed and transported by agents of the Institute and insured for any value you may set upon it.

The exhibition of the Carnegie lasts from Nov. 5 to Jan. 1.

Please let me know promptly if the picture may be exhibited.

Yours truly,
Thomas Eakins

56   John Singer SARGENT (1856-1925)

Dr. Pozzi at Home, 1881
Oil on canvas: 80 1/2″ x 43 7/8″ (204.5 x 111.5 cm.)
Signed and dated upper right: John S. Sargent, 1881

Collection: Estate of the Hon. Jean Pozzi (Sale, Paris, Palais Gallièra, Dec. 4, 1970, no. 84, repr. also on cat. cover in color)

Exhibitions: See catalog ref. page
First Exhibited: VIII
Not Exhibited: XX
Exhibited: Los Angeles, Los Angeles County Museum of Art, on exhibition, *American Paintings,* Aug. 6-Dec. 9, 1974

Literature: *L'Art et les Artistes,* vol. IV (1905-1907), p. 368, repr.; William Howe Downes, *John S. Sargent, His Life and Work,* Boston: Little, Brown & Company, 1925, pp. 10-11, 113; Hon. Evan Charteris, *John Sargent,* New York; Charles Scribner's Sons, 1927, p. 258; Charles Merrill Mount, *John Singer Sargent,* London: The Cresset Press, 1957, pp. 61-65, 67, 69, 116, 153; Richard Ormond, *John Singer Sargent, Paintings, Drawings, Watercolors,* New York: Harper & Row, 1970, p. 34; Sale catalog, *Tableaux Modernes, Sculptures,* Paris: Palais Gallièra, Dec. 4, 1970, no. 84, repr., also on cat. cover in color

---

While there was still a decidedly youthful quality in Sargent's work in 1881, he was rapidly reaching full stride as an artist. Already honored in the Salon of 1879 for the dramatic portrait of his teacher, Carolus-Duran, in 1881 he received a medal second class, making him "...*hors concours* and a great swell," as he jokingly put it. The portrait of *Dr. Pozzi at Home* was eagerly undertaken by an artist brimming with enthusiasm and confidence.

Innovative from the beginning, Sargent was never content with a formal, straightforward likeness. Even in the early portrait of Carolus, the teacher assumes a special vitality in a dynamic pose conveying force and movement. It was perhaps the influence of Impressionism that led him to ask Mme. Pailleron to pose standing out of doors when he painted the full-length standing portrait which appeared in the Salon of 1880. Some of his greatest portraits are the most informal ones, catching the subject engaged in life, as it were; the portrait of Dr. Pozzi is a powerful statement of this kind. Moving beyond the snapshot effect which could so easily result from this approach, the artist brings to the painting much more than the experience of Carolus' studio. Certainly, the solid grasp of form and light, particularly in the head, reflects the method of his teacher, but Sargent's own personal gift, expanded and refined by a close study of the old masters, is affirmed. The drama of the painting is an extension of the artist's response to the work of Velàsquez and Hals which he had studied so closely in previous months. In gesture and movement the figure is purely Baroque, and, despite the overt drama of the technically superb glazes, there is a subtlety of light and tone which could have had its source in Velàsquez.

57 John Singer SARGENT (1856-1925)

Portrait of Mrs. Edward L. Davis and Her Son, Livingston Davis, 1890
Oil on canvas: 86″ x 48″ (218.4 x 121.9 cm.)
Signed lower right: John S. Sargent

Collections: Edward Livingston Davis, Worcester, Mass.; Livingston Davis, Boston, Mass.; Mrs. A. Winsor Weld, Boston, Mass. (Sale, New York, Parke-Bernet Galleries, Inc., Mar. 19-20, 1969, no. 74); James Graham & Sons, New York; Los Angeles County Museum of Art, (Frances and Armand Hammer Purchase Fund, 1969)

Exhibited: New York, National Academy of Design, 1890; New York, Society of American Artists, 1891; Boston, Massachusetts, Boston Art Museum, 1891; Chicago, Illinois, *World's Columbian Exhibition,* 1893, no. 875; Boston, Massachusetts, Copley Hall, *Loan Collection of Portraits of Women,* 1895, no. 257; Philadelphia, Pennsylvania, Pennsylvania Academy of the Fine Arts, 1896; Boston, Massachusetts, Copley Hall, *Paintings and Sketches by John S. Sargent, R. A.,* Feb. 20-Mar. 13, 1899, no. 5; Worcester, Massachusetts, Worcester Art Museum, 1909; Boston, Massachusetts, Museum of Fine Arts; 1913, no. 757; 1916 no. 573; 1918, no. 480; 1920, no. 340; 1921, no. 420; New York, Grand Central Art Galleries, *Retrospective Exhibition of Important Works of John Singer Sargent,* Feb. 23-Apr. 6, 1924, no. 20 (repr. in cat. p. 45); New York, The Metropolitan Museum of Art, *Memorial Exhibition of the Works of John Singer Sargent,* Jan. 4-Feb. 14, 1926, no. 26 (repr. in cat.); Boston, Massachusetts, Museum of Fine Arts: 1928, no. 168; 1929, no. 993; 1930, no. 530; 1956, no. 20; Idem, Centennial Exhibition, *Sargent's Boston,* Jan. 3-Feb. 7, 1956

Exhibitions: See catalog ref. page
First Exhibited: II
Not Exhibited: IV, V, VI, VII, IX, X, XIII, XX, XXIII
Exhibited: Los Angeles, Los Angeles County Museum of Art, on exhibition, *American Paintings,* Aug. 6-Dec. 9, 1974

Literature: Leila Machlin, "The Sargent Exhibition," *The American Magazine of Art,* vol. XV, no. 4, Apr. 1924, pp. 169-190, repr. p. 184; Rose V. S. Berry, "John Singer Sargent: Some of His American Work," *Art and Archaeology throughout the Ages,* vol. XVIII, no. 3, Sept. 1924, pp. 83-112, repr. p. 100; William Howe Downes, *John S. Sargent, His Life and Work,* Boston, Little, Brown & Co., 1925, pp. 33, 157-158, repr. p. 128; Evan Charteris, *John S. Sargent,* New York: Charles Scribner's Sons, 1927, pp. 109, 137, 263; Charles Merrill Mount, *John Singer Sargent,* New York: W. W. Norton, 1955, pp. 183, 433, no. 9024; David McKibbin *Sargent's Boston,* Boston, Museum of Fine Arts, 1956, pp. 43, 68, 91, repr. p. 41; Sale catalog, *18th-20th Century American Paintings, etc.—Various Owners,* New York: Parke-

Bernet Galleries, Mar. 19-20, 1969, no. 74, repr.; Richard Ormond, *John Singer Sargent, Paintings, Drawings, Watercolors,* New York: Harper & Row, 1970, pp. 43, 246, repr.

By 1889 when Sargent came to this country to discuss the mural project for the Boston Public Library, he was already the most renowned portrait painter of his day. When he was not actually involved with plans for the murals, portrait commissions in New York and Boston kept him completely absorbed. It is typical of the artist that moving about from one country to another and from one city to the next did not interfere with his work nor impair its quality.

The portrait of *Mrs. Edward L. Davis and her Son, Livingston Davis,* painted, according to Downes, in the family's coach house, is not a simple bust portrait but an imposing composition demanding the artist's full powers of invention and execution. For Sargent the inherent challenge becomes inspiration, and the figures of the full-length double portrait spring to life almost spontaneously.

The seemingly casual relationship between the two figures is actually a relationship of considerable formal and psychological complexity. The precarious movement of the boy is played against the monumentally stable form of his mother who looms forward as she forcefully confronts the viewer. While the broad, loose brushwork continues to reflect Sargent's debt to the Dutch and Spanish masters and even to an extent to the Impressionists, the firm modeling and dramatic lighting of the woman's head seem to have something of the quality of the realist Copley, whose work Sargent discovered in Boston.

58   Mary CASSATT (1844-1926)

Summertime, 1894
Oil on canvas: 28 7/8″ x 39 3/8″ (73.4 x 100.0 cm.)
Signed lower right: Mary Cassatt

Collection: Huntington Hartford, New York (Sale, New York, Parke-Bernet Galleries, Inc., May 10, 1971, no. 28)

Exhibited: Baltimore, Maryland, Baltimore Museum of Art, *Manet, Degas, Berthe Morisot and Mary Cassatt,* Apr. 18-June 3, 1962, no. 116 (lent by Huntington Hartford); St. Petersburg, Florida, Museum of Fine Arts, *Inaugural Exhibition,* Feb. 7-Mar. 7, 1965, no. 28 (lent by Huntington Hartford); New York, M. Knoedler & Co., *Mary Cassatt,* Feb. 1-Feb. 26, 1966, no. 25 (lent by Huntington Hartford); Southampton, Long Island, New York. The Parrish Art Museum, *Miss Mary Cassatt, Paintings and the Graphic Arts,* July 30-Aug. 20, 1967, no. 2 (lent by Huntington Hartford); Washington, D.C., National Gallery of Art, *Mary Cassatt,*

Sept. 27-Nov. 8, 1970, no. 55, p. 28 (repr. in cat.) (lent by Huntington Hartford)

Exhibitions: See catalog ref. page
First Exhibited: IX
Not Exhibited: XVII, XVIII, XIX, XX
Exhibited: Washington, D.C., National Gallery of Art, *American Impressionists Exhibition,* May 6-Aug. 12, 1973; New York, Whitney Museum of American Art, *American Impressionists Exhibition,* Sept. 18-Nov. 12, 1973; Cincinnati, Ohio, Cincinnati Museum of Art, *American Impressionists Exhibition,* Dec. 15, 1973-Jan. 31, 1974; Raleigh, North Carolina, North Carolina Museum of Art, *American Impressionists Exhibition,* Mar. 8-Apr. 29, 1974; Los Angeles, Los Angeles County Museum of Art, on exhibition, *American Paintings,* Aug. 6-Dec. 9, 1974; Manila, National Museum of Manila, Oct. 2, 1976

Literature: Adelyn Dohme Breeskin, *Mary Cassatt, A Catalogue Raisonné of the Oils, Pastels, Watercolors, and Drawings,* Washington, D.C.: Smithsonian Institution Press, 1970, no. 240, p. 116, repr.; Meryle Secrest, "The American Impressionist, The Lyrical Mary Cassatt Goes on Exhibit in Washington." *The Washington Post,* Sept. 20, 1970, Section KI, repr. in color; Sale catalog, *Important Impressionist and Modern Paintings and Drawings,* New York: Parke-Bernet Galleries, Inc., May 10, 1971, no. 28, p. 50, repr. in color

---

Though Mary Cassatt's paintings are generally more or less complex figure compositions, she remains essentially a portrait painter concentrating on the likeness and character of individuals. As a rule even when she painted figures engaged in some activity out of doors, she remained as much concerned with portraiture as with the disposition of form and features within a pictorial space. Among the few exceptions are three boating scenes from 1893-1894 (Breeskin 230, 233 and 240). In none of these are the subjects identified, but in the famous *The Boating Party (Near Antibes),* 1893, the personalities emerge with great strength. In the other two, which are closely related, the identity of the figures is not an important factor, and the intention seems to be simply the creation of a plein-air-view of figures in a boat observing or feeding ducks.

A number of important factors entered into the conception of *Summertime.* As early as 1890 Cassatt had resolved to concentrate on strengthening form and drawing, much as Renoir did in mid-career, and the following year a series of prints emulating the Japanese had a profound effect on her style. This is obvious in *The Boating Party,* but while boldness of design is still very important in *Summertime,* it is augmented by a system of slashing, dynamic brushwork verging on abstraction. Interestingly, the large allegory commissioned for the Chicago World's Fair and painted in 1892 also included women and ducks in a landscape.

59 Maurice Brazil PRENDERGAST (1861-1924)

On the Beach, 1916
Oil on canvas: 26 3/4" x 39" (67.9 x 99.0 cm.)

Collections: Mrs. Charles Prendergast, Westport, Conn.; Lester Avnet, New York; A.C.A. Galleries, New York

Exhibited: Pittsburgh, Pennsylvania, Museum of Art, Carnegie Institute, *The 23rd Annual International Exhibition of Paintings,* Apr. 24-June 15, 1924, no. 14; Hartford, Connecticut, Wadsworth Athenaeum, *Connecticut Collections,* Oct. 1957; Stamford, Connecticut, Stamford Museum and Nature Center, Nov. 1961; New York, A.C.A. Galleries, *Lester Avnet Collection,* Sept. 18-Oct. 18, 1969

Exhibitions: See catalog ref. page
First Exhibited: VII
Not Exhibited: XX, XXIII
Exhibited: Los Angeles, Los Angeles County Museum of Art, on exhibition, *American Paintings,* Aug. 6-Dec. 9, 1974

Literature: *Catalogue of the 23rd Annual International Exhibition of Paintings,* Carnegie Institute Press, 1924, no. 14

———————————

Unlike many of his contemporaries, Prendergast did not embrace the more conservative aspects of Impressionism. Rather, from the beginning he struck out in a direction close to that of the Post-Impressionists and Nabis. Later, there were even stylistic parallels with the Fauves.

Typical of Prendergast's later painting in oil this work exhibits nothing of the Realist doctrine generally associated with other members of the Eight group. His subjects were not the crowded streets of the New York slums painted by the Ashcan School, but groups of happy people at their leisure on the beach, in the park, thronging the sunny boulevards of Paris or the bridges of Venice. Figures are generally disposed laterally across the foreground against highly simplified forms of sea and land. The ultimate result is a bright, lyrical tapestry of color with shapes loosely defined by a heavy line breaking or fading against shifting planes of color as it approximates contour.

60 Andrew WYETH (1917-   )

Brandywine Valley, 1940
Watercolor: 21" x 29" (53.3 x 73.7 cm.)

Signed and dated lower right: Andrew Wyeth 1940
Painted at the John Chad house in Chaddsford, Pennsylvania

Exhibitions: See catalog ref. page
First Exhibited: III
Not Exhibited: X, XX, XXIII

Literature: Sale catalog, *Impressionist, American and Modern Paintings and Watercolors,* Houston, Texas: Christie, Manson & Woods (New York), Apr. 6, 1970, no. 21, p. 19

———————————

In contrast to the structure and design of Wyeth's more recent works in drybrush, which have much in common with his tempera paintings, the freely flowing washes of this early example take every advantage of the inherent qualities of transparent watercolor.

The lessons found in the work of such artists as Winslow Homer and the rigorous tutelage of his father helped Wyeth to develop absolute mastery of the medium at an early age. This watercolor, painted more than thirty years ago, reveals his deep involvement with the Brandywine Valley where he still lives and works without regard for contemporary trends in the United States or abroad.

61 Albrecht DÜRER (1471-1528)

Tuft of Cowslips
Gouache on vellum: 7 9/16" x 6 5/8" (19.2 x 16.8 cm.)
Signed (in later hand): AD; Dated (in another hand): 1526

Collections: Private collection, England; Hal O'Nians, London

Exhibitions: See catalog ref. page
First Exhibited: XI
Not Exhibited: XX, XXIII
Exhibited: Washington, D.C., National Gallery of Art, on exhibition, June 2-Sept. 1, 1974; Los Angeles, Los Angeles County Museum of Art, *Old Master Drawing Show,* Apr. 29-June 8, 1976

Literature: Jaro Springer, "Dürers Zeichnungen in neuen Publikationen," *Repertorium für Kunstwissenschaft,* 29, 1906, p. 555ff.; Joseph Meder, "Die grüne Passion und die Tier— und Pflanzenstudien Albrecht Dürers in der Albertina *Repertorium für Kunstwissenschaft,* 30, 1907, p. 181; Sebastian Killermann," A. Dürers Pflanzen und Tierzeichnungen," *Studien zur deutschen Kunstgeschichte* 119, Strassburg, 1910, pp. 94ff.; Friedrich Winkler, *Die Zeichnungen Albrecht Dürers,* Berlin, 1936, II, p. 65ff.; Heinrich Schwartz, "A Water-colour attributed to Dürer," *The Burlington Magazine* 95, 1953, p. 149ff.; Hans Kauffmann, "Dürer in der Kunst und im Kunsturteil um 1600," *Anzeiger des Germanischen Nationalmuseums in Nürnberg,* 1940-1953, 1954, p. 29; Otto Benesch, *Master Drawings in the Albertina,* New York: 1967, p. 337; Charles W. Talbot, ed., *Dürer in America—His Graphic Work,* Washington, D.C.: The National Gallery of Art, 1971, p. 110, note 3

———————

Until recently when the *Tuft of Cowslips* was purchased for the Hammer Collection, the only plant study in this country credited to Albrecht Dürer was the *Buttercup* given by Mrs. Charles Bradley to the Museum of Art at the Rhode Island School of Design. The Rhode Island drawing forms an integral part of a group of three more sheets, the *Columbine,* the *Celandine* and the *Three Medicinal Herbs,* all at the Albertina in Vienna, from which, in fact, the *Buttercup* had been separated during the Napoleonic wars. Similar in technique and style, all four have in common that they are painted on vellum, mostly with smooth and opaque goache; that they depict wild-growing plants; that a patch of soil is represented together with the plants; and that a later collector's hand, not Dürer's, has added the date 1526 in each case. In addition, the *Small Piece of Turf*—also in the Albertina—although undated, is extremely close in style. The date 1526 can also be found on a drawing in Berlin of two cut peonies. Although this drawing is also painted on vellum, it is somewhat different in style.

Most of these flower pieces can be clearly identified with drawings acquired after 1588 by Emperor Rudolf II in Prague from Anna Imhoff in Nuremberg. The Imhoffs had bought many of them in 1560 from the widow of Endres Dürer, Albrecht's brother, but the Imhoff family also bought from other sources (e.g., from the heirs of Paul Koler), so that this provenance does not guarantee absolute authenticity. In fact, Dürer's authorship of all of these drawings has been doubted by scholars, but no satisfactory alternative has yet been found. The work of the Dürer imitator, Hans Hoffmann, active in Nuremberg in the second half of the Sixteenth Century (in time to slip his works into the Imhoff Collection before its sale to the Emperor), seems to be quite different, as Hans Kauffmann has explained so well. Like Joseph Meder and Otto Benesch, the directors of the Albertina, Hans Kauffmann can be counted among the defenders of Dürer's authorship for the group.

The immediacy of observation from life is expressed in these plant studies by the patches of soil and by the representation of accidental weeds and grasses together with the flowers. This trait they share only with some of the plants in the paintings of great Netherlandish artists like Hugo van der Goes or with the only surely accepted plant study by Dürer, the *Great Piece of Turf,* also in the Albertina in Vienna and dated 1503 by Dürer himself.

The *Great Piece of Turf,* painted on paper mainly in watercolor with only some touches of gouache, not only has a greater transparency of color but also more emphasis on line in shading and contour. For these reasons it is comparable to several studies, all painted on paper, of single, cut garden flowers in Bremen and elsewhere. If one accepts Dürer's authorship for both groups, technique may be one of the reasons for the differences between them. But the differences might also be explained by different dates of execution.

There is another, still somewhat different, drawing in the Albertina, the small *Nosegay of Violets.* Painted on vellum and very likely identical to one in the Imhoff list, it is done in a somewhat coarser, freer gouache, at least in the treatment of the leaves.

The newcomer to these plant studies, the *Tuft of Cowslips,* is interesting in many ways. It is painted on vellum with some watercolor and more gouache, and, as do most of the vellum group, it bears the date 1526. At one time, therefore, it must have belonged to the same collection. The dark color of the patch of soil is also closely related to the rest of the group. The color of the leaves, however, totally lacks the smoothness of the leaves of the vellum group and is much more lively and more transparently applied. In fact, when closely compared, the highly differentiated greens of the *Tuft of Cowslips* seem to correspond almost exactly to those in the the *Great Piece of Turf.* In particular, the strong light green of the highlights on the leaves of the foreground is absolutely identical to the most strident green in the work in the Albertina. On the other hand, the loose application of just these touches is most closely related to the execution of the leaves of the bunch of violets in the same collection. Although the *Tuft of Cowslips* has none of the linear quality typical of the paper group, it corresponds to the *Great Piece of Turf* in the spatial depth, in the richness of the observation of light, and in the life emanating from the plant. The tender trefoil of clover appearing in the center amidst the thicker leaves of the cowslip illustrates both the delicacy of the artist's technique and his refinements of observation. The velvety, rich surfaces of some of the leaves farther back is equally strong testimony for the drawings having been created by an artist of the highest standards.

The Hammer drawing thus offers a new perspective on the whole group of flower pieces. An artist like Dürer, whose means vary with the object and with his objectives, and whose watercolors of landscape include the miniature-like density of his view of Innsbruck, the impressionistic looseness of his view of the valley near Kalkreuth, and the graphic clarity of the wooden covered bridge called *Trockensteg* in his native Nuremberg, can well be credited with different methods of executing plants. The *Tuft of Cowslips* may well be the centerpiece which ties the three different groups together. In spatial richness and liveliness and in delicacy of color, it is far closer than any other of the vellum group to the *Great Piece of Turf*.

The Hammer drawing was, in fact, taken to the Albertina and there put side by side with the *Great Piece of Turf*. After intense study, the curators of the Albertina, including Dr. Walter Koschatzky, Dr. Alice Strobl, and Dr. Konrad Oberhuber, were all convinced that the Hammer drawing was undoubtedly by the same hand that created the *Great Piece of Turf*.

62 LEONARDO da VINCI (1452-1519)

Sheet of Studies: head of an old man in profile to right; two detailed studies of the right eye; bust of a woman from three-quarter rear with head in profile to right; bust of a girl from three-quarter rear with head turned toward viewer
Pen and brown ink over traces of black chalk
6 1/2″ x 5 1/2″ (16.4 x 13.8 cm.)

Verso: sketches in black chalk
Paper watermarked with a tulip (cf. Briquet, *Les Filigranes, Dictionnaire Historique des Marques du Papier*, 1907, vol. 2, cat. nos. 6645-6659)

Collection: P. & D. Colnaghi, London, England

Exhibitions: See catalog ref. page
First Exhibited: XIII
Not Exhibited: XX, XXIII
Exhibited: Washington, D.C. *National Gallery of Art, National Gallery Exhibition*, June 2-Sept. 1, 1974; Los Angeles, Los Angeles County Museum of Art, *Old Master Drawing Show*, Apr. 29-June 8, 1976

Accepted as original of Leonardo da Vinci by Lord (Kenneth) Clark, James Byam Shaw of Christ Church, Oxford, and Christopher White and Konrad Oberhuber of the National Gallery, Washington, D.C., this drawing compares closely to a sheet of studies in the collection of H. M. Queen Elizabeth II at Windsor Castle (Kenneth Clark, *A Catalogue of the Drawings of Leonardo da Vinci in the Collection of His Majesty the King at Windsor Castle*, Cambridge: The University Press, 1935, cat. no. 12276 verso repr.) dated ca. 1478-1480. Byam Shaw compares it to a drawing in the collection of Count Antoine Seilern in London (*Italian Paintings and Drawings at 56, Princess Gate, London, S. W. 7*, London: Shenval Press, 1959, cat. no. 80 repr.) dated ca. 1480.

63 MICHELANGELO BUONARROTI (1475-1564)

Male Nude (recto)
Male Nude (verso)
Black chalk: 9 1/4″ x 4″ (23.3 x 10.0 cm.)

Collections: Sir J. C. Robinson; John Malcolm; The Hon. A. E. Gathorne-Hardy; Geoffrey Gathorne-Hardy; The Hon. Robert Gathorne-Hardy

Exhibited: London, British Museum, *Michelangelo*, 1953, no. 128; Manchester, *Between Renaissance and Baroque*, 1965, no. 338; London, P. & D. Colnaghi, *Loan Exhibition...*, 1971, no. 9, pl. VII and afterwards at the Ashmolean Museum, Oxford; London, British Museum, *Drawings by Michelangelo*, 1975, no. 156, repr.

Exhibitions: See catalog ref. page
First Exhibited: XXIX
Exhibited: Los Angeles, Los Angeles County Museum of Art, *Old Master Drawing Show*, April 29-June 9, 1976

Literature: Gathorne-Hardy catalogue no. 7; Bernard Berenson, *The Drawings of the Florentine Painters*, 1903, vol. II, no. 1540; Henry Thode, *Michelangelo, Kritische Untersuchungen*, Berlin, 1913, p. 163, no. 368; Bernard Berenson, *The Drawings of the Florentine Painters*, 1938, vol. II, no. 1544b, repr. fig. 717; Johannes Wilde, *Italian Drawings...in the British Museum, Michelangelo and his Studio*, 1953, under cat. no. 75, p. 116, Bernard Berenson, *I disegni dei pittori florentini*, 1961, vol. II, no. 1544b; L. Dussler, *Die Zeichnungen des Michelangelo*, Berlin, 1959, no. 338, pl. 136; Charles de Tolnay, *Michelangelo, The Final Period*, 1960, p. 206, cat. no. 219, pl. 197; Frederick Hartt, *The Drawings of Michelangelo*, 1971, cat. no. 509, repr.; Paul Joannides, *The Burlington Magazine*, review of exhibition *Drawings by Michelangelo* at the British Museum, April, 1975, p. 262

This study is linked with the third and fourth group from the left in the Ashmolean *Studies for a Pietà*, which John Gere and Nicholas Turner in the B. M. exhibition catalogue tentatively suggest 'might have been the germ of the (Rondanini) Pietà.' For a direct comparison both drawings are reproduced side by side.

64 RAPHAEL SANZIO (1483-1520)

Study for a Fresco with Hosea and Jonah
Pen and brown wash, heightened with white over preparation in black chalk and stylus, squared with stylus and red chalk
10 5/8″ x 7 13/16″ (26.2 x 19.8 cm.)

Collections: J. Richardson, Sr.; J. Richardson, Jr., London (Frits Lugt, *Marque des Collections*, no. 2170); P. J. Mariette,

Paris (Lugt 2097); H. C. Jennings, London (Lugt 2771);
P. Payne Knight; Baron H. de Triquety, Paris (Lugt 1304);
E. Colando, Paris (Lugt 837); Major S. V. Christie-Miller
C.B.E.

Exhibitions: See catalog ref. page
First Exhibited: XI
Not Exhibited: XX, XXIII
Exhibited: Washington, D.C., National Gallery of Art,
National Gallery Exhibition, June 2-Sept. 1, 1974; Los Angeles,
Los Angeles County Museum of Art, *Old Master Drawing
Show,* Apr. 29-June 8, 1976

Literature: Jonathan Richardson, *An Account of the Statues,
Bas-Reliefs, Drawings and Pictures in Italy, France, etc., with
remarks by Mr. Richardson, Sen. and Jun. (2nd ed.),* London,
1754, p. 104; C. Metz, *Imitations of Ancient and Modern
Drawings,* London, 1798, pl. XXXXIV; J. D. Passavant,
Raphäel d'Urbin, Paris, 1860, vol. II, p. 142; F. A. Gruyer,
Raphäel et l'Antiquité, Paris, 1846, vol. I, p. 379, no. 1;
C. Ruland, *The Works of Raphael Santi da Urbino As
Represented in the Raphael Collection in the Royal Library at
Windsor Castle,* London, 1876, p. 271, vol. III, 4; J. A.
Crowe and G. B. Cavalcaselle, *Raphael, Life and Works,*
London, 1882-85, vol. II, p. 216, note; G. E. Lafenestre and
E. Richtenberger, *Rome, Le Vatican et les Eglises,* Paris,
1903, p. 263; Oskar Fischel, "Some Lost Drawings By or
Near Raphael," *The Burlington Magazine,* 20, 1912, p. 299,
pl. II, fig. 12; Oskar Fischel, under "Santi," in Thieme-
Becker, *Allgemeines Lexikon der Bildenden Künstler* 29,
1935, p. 438; Oskar Fischel, *Raphael, A Critical Catalogue
of His Pictures, Wall-Paintings and Tapestries,* London,
1971, p. 94

In the winter of 1510-1511 Pope Julius II was absent from Rome for a considerable time. We know that during this period Michelangelo did not progress with his work on the Sistine ceiling for lack of funds, and it is highly probable that Raphael encountered similar difficulties. Very likely it was at that time that Agostino Chigi, the rich Sienese banker and one of the greatest patrons of Renaissance Rome, commissioned Raphael to design and partly execute the decoration of his chapel in the church of Santa Marie della Pace in Rome. All that was painted were the prophets high on the walls flanking the window in the lunette about the cornice and the sibyls on the face of the arch below the cornice and above the altar niche. Because these were the most accessible frescoes by the great master, they were among his most admired creations. Over the centuries, unfortunately, the condition of the frescoes has deteriorated. The prophets are overpainted; the sibyls, although restored, have lost some of their original freshness. As a result, their fame has been eclipsed by the Stanze, well-presented and now readily accessible as part of the Vatican Museums.

Since the prophets high above the cornice are difficult to decipher from below, the Hammer drawing is of special value in giving us an idea of this great work. It represents the group at the left of the window, Jonah and Hosea, both predicting, as all the other seers do, the Resurrection of Christ and of the dead. The drawing is finished to a large degree. As indicated by the drawings preserved for the pendant, the figures of the prophets must have been prepared in many small sketches and in detailed studies after the model. In fact, Raphael squared the paper with a stylus to facilitate his drawing the figures of the prophets in exact scale. He drew first in black chalk and then with pen. While the ink was still partially wet on the right side, he washed in the shadows with large and rapid touches of the brush and then added the white highlights which give such great life to Jonah's face. These grand, finished figures recall both the philosophers of the School of Athens that Raphael had painted only a short time before and Michelangelo's ideas for the tomb of Julius II, with which Raphael must have been familiar.

Quite different from the prophets is the figure of the angel, rapidly sketched in with a freer pen over some preparation with the stylus. Only the most important shading is added. We know from early sketches that this angel was originally placed in a slightly different, much more hidden position, behind Jonah. He is now given greater prominence. As is customary with Raphael, the figure is drawn in the nude to give a better idea of the movement. The angel differs, therefore, from the work as executed where he wears a cloak around his thigh. Raphael had second thoughts about the angel's left arm. It was at first lightly indicated somewhat higher than it appears in the final version. When the drawing was finished, Raphael covered it with another net of lines in red chalk to transfer it, probably directly, to the cartoon. But for some minor changes and the exceptions noted here, the fresco corresponds very closely to the drawing.

None of the authors who have written about the drawing in recent times have had the opportunity to see it, and most of the older authors knew it only from the facsimile done by Metz. Fischel, publishing the old photo in Windsor Castle, was at first hesitant to pass judgment but later seems to have thought that the drawing was by Giulio Romano. This idea was possible only because he dated the fresco 1514, when Giulio was already active. Dussler judging exclusively from Fischel's reproduction, gave it more generally to the School of Raphael, knowing well that in 1511 Giulio was too young to have done such a work. However, no serious activity is recorded for any of the other members of Raphael's school at that time, and the insight into the creative process that the drawing affords precludes any possibility of regarding it as a copy. In fact, as James Byam Shaw has commented, when the drawing is seen in the original, its quality makes it abundantly clear that only Raphael could have been the author. It corresponds well to other of Raphael's drawings for the Stanza della Segnatura. In fact, in its combination of highly finished parts and loosely drawn sections, it must be considered among the most representative of Raphael's drawings of that period. It will be included in volume 10 of *Raphaels Zeichnungen,* begun in 1913 by Oskar Fischel and continued at present by Konrad Oberhuber.

65   Andrea del SARTO (1486-1530)

Female Head
Black chalk, 12 7/8″ x 8 7/8″ (32.7 x 22.5 cm.)
Signed lower left: A. del Sarto

Collections: Jan Pietersz.Zoomer, Amsterdam (1641-1724) (Lugt. 1511); Jonathan Richardson Sen., London (1665-1745), (Lugt. 2184); Duke of Argyll (by 1784; Sale at T. Philipe's, London, May 21-23, 1798); Walter Savage Landor

Exhibitions: See catalog ref. page
First Exhibited: XXXIV

Literature: John Shearman, *Andrea del Sarto,* Oxford, 1965, p. 385f., pl. 47a.

66   Antonio Allegri, da CORREGGIO (1494-1534)

Pendentive Study with Sts. Matthew and Jerome (recto)
Ink and red chalk: 8 1/4″ x 5 1/2″ (21.0 x 14.0)
Study for the "Madonna della Scodella" (verso)
Ink and red chalk: 7 15/16″ x 5″ (20.2 x 12.7 cm.)

Collections: Sir Peter Lely, London; P. and D. Colnaghi & Co., Ltd., London; Michael Hirst, London

Exhibited: Edinburgh, The Arts Council of Scotland, *Exhibitions of Italian 16th Century Drawings from British Private Collections,* Aug. 1969

Exhibitions: See catalog ref. page
First Exhibited: VIII
Not Exhibited: X, XX, XXIII
Exhibited: Washington, D.C., National Gallery of Art, National Gallery Exhibit, June 2—Sept. 1, 1974

Literature: Konrad Oberhuber, "Drawings by Artists Working in Parma in the Sixteenth Century," *Master Drawings,* vol. VIII, no. 3, 1970, pp. 278-279, pl. 30 (recto), pl. 31 (verso)

This double sheet has been fully published by Konrad Oberhuber in a review of A. E. Popham's *Italian Drawings in the Department of Prints and Drawings in the British Museum, Artists Working in Parma in the Sixteenth Century,* 1967, which appeared in *Master Drawings,* vol. VIII, no. 3, 1970, pp. 278-279.

According to Dr. Oberhuber's analysis, these studies are the earliest by the artist so far known for the two works listed above. This accounts for the changes, as well as the divergences, from the final versions and the rudeness of the draftmanship.

Several other preliminary drawings exist for the pendentive fresco, but the verso of the Hammer sheet is apparently one of only two known sketches for the altarpiece, the *Rest on the Flight into Egypt,* also called the *Madonna della Scodella* ("Madonna with the plate"), dated 1530, which is now in the Gallery of Parma. The other sketch, which is now in the Uffizi, was considered a copy by Corrado Ricci but was accepted as genuine by A. E. Popham (*Correggio's Drawings,* 1957, cat. no. 76).

Although the majority of Correggio's drawings were executed in natural red chalk, he sometimes enforced this medium with pen and ink (to increase the definition of the form) beyond that of his initial sketch. Correggio was not a beautiful or polished draftsman in the same sense, for example, as were Leonardo or Raphäel. He was largely self-taught in the art of drawing, and he used the medium chiefly to work out facets of his paintings and frecoes. Lineal grace and rhythm were not his concerns as his approach was painterly rather than graphic. The various stages of his drawings as he developed and altered his ideas for compositions are reflected in their varying techniques. Some are broad in execution and well-defined, others composed of numerous alterations are re-drawing in the search for their final form. The present double sheet is an example of the latter type. It is perhaps less characteristic of the artist than his better known, pure chalk drawings, but in its technique and re-work it agrees with several of his other designs. The contouring of the figures of the *Madonna della Scodella* study, for example, is similar to that found on the recto of the Louvre drawing of several *putti* (Popham 28). The Louvre drawing relates to the artist's fresco in the apse of S. Giovanni Evangelista.

67   REMBRANDT van Rijn (1606-1669)

A Biblical Subject
Pen and ink, brown wash, heightened with white
6 13/16″ x 6 3/4″ (17.3 x 17.2 cm.)
Watermark: Arms of Amsterdam
Collection: B. F. Nicholson (Sale, London, Sotheby & Co., Mar. 23, 1971, no. 90)

Exhibitions: See catalog ref. page
First Exhibited: IX
Not Exhibited: X, XX, XXIII
Exhibited: Washington, D.C., National Gallery of Art,
National Gallery Exhibition, June 2-Sept. 1, 1974; Los Angeles,
Los Angeles County Museum of Art, *Old Master Drawing
Show*, Apr. 29-June 13, 1976

An elderly king, wearing a turban surmounted by a
crown, and holding a sceptre in his right hand, is
seated on a throne beneath a baldachin. On the right,
two female figures kneel side by side before him. T
woman on the left clasps something on her knee.

The king is similar in type to the artist's representation
of Biblical kings, such as David, in the drawing of
Nathan Admonishing David, ca. 1655, in the
Metropolitan Museum (Benesch 948). He also bears
a strong affinity to a number of the figures in the copies
Rembrandt made after Moghul miniatures in the
mid-1650's (Benesch 1187-1206), suggesting that the
artist drew inspiration from these for his representation
of an Old Testament figure.

The subject is not easily elucidated. The suggested
identification of the Judgment of Solomon, made in the
sale catalog, is not entirely convincing. In the first
place, it is by no means certain that the woman on the
left holds a baby. The object could equally well be a
jar. Secondly, the position of the second woman
suggests that she is an attendant and not a rival. The
scene depicted here must represent a woman humbly
making some offering to an elderly king.

This sheet, which until its recent appearance in the
sale room was unknown, is comparable to a number of
late Rembrandt drawings, in particular *Isaac and
Rebecca Spied Upon by Abimelach,* in a private
collection, New York (Benesch 988), which has been
variously dated in the late 1650's or early 1660's (for a
discussion of this drawing which favors the latter
dating, see *Rembrandt Drawings from American
Collections,* Pierpont Morgan Library, Fogg Art
Museum, 1960, no. 76). The delineation of the couple
in this study is notably similar to that of the two
kneeling women in the present sheet.

68 REMBRANDT van Rijn (1606-1669)

Studies of a Beggar Man and Woman
Pen and brown ink: 5" x 4 3/8" (12.7 x 11.1 cm.)

Collections: Jonathan Richardson Sen. (L. 2183), his
attribution 'Rembrandt' transferred to new mount; Sir Joshua
Reynolds (L. 2364): Sir Thomas Lawrence (L. 2445); William
Esdaile (L. 2617); Christie's, 17th June, 1840, lot 4 (/-to
Sheath); Sir Archibald Campbell Bt., and thence by descent
to Sir Ilay Campbell Bt.

Exhibitions: See catalog ref. page
First Exhibited: XXXII

Literature: A. M. Hind, *Vasari Society,* 1908-09, lst series,
Pt. IV. No. 26; K. Bauch, *Die Kunst des jungen Rembrandts,*
1933, p. 204, fig. 111; O. Benesch, *The Drawings of
Rembrandt,* 1954, Vol. II, No. 206, fig. 223 and 1973, Vol.
II, No. 206, fig. 241

Though Bauch held that this drawing is of the early
Leiden period, it is dated by Benesch about 1632, who
compares it with another study of a beggar in the
Rijksprentenkabinet (see Benesch, op. cit. 1954,
No. 205).

69 Antoine WATTEAU (1684-1721)

Young Girl
Red and black chalk: 8 1/2" x 5 3/4" (21.6 x 14.6 cm)

Collections: Philippe Wiener, Paris; Albert Meyer (Sale,
Paris, May 24-June 8, 1935, no. 100); Mrs. Jesse I. Straus,
New York

Exhibited: London, Royal Academy of Arts, *The London
Exhibition of French Art, 1200-1900,* Jan.-Mar. 1932, no. 713,
cat. no. 765 (lent by Albert Meyer); Paris, Jean A. Seligmann,
Collection Albert Meyer, May 24-June 8, 1935, no. 100

Exhibitions: See catalog ref. page
First Exhibited: VII
Not Exhibited: XX, XXIII

Literature: Edmond de Goncourt, *Catalogue Raisonné de
l'Oeuvre Peint, Dessiné et Gravé d'Antoine Watteau,* Paris:
Rapilly, 1875, no. 652, p. 297; Seymour de Ricci, *Catalogue
de Dessins de Maîtres du XVIIIème Siècle, Collection Albert
Meyer,* Paris: Jean A. Seligmann, 1935, no. 100, repr. opp.;
*Commemorative Catalogue of the London Exhibition of
French Art, 1200-1900,* London: Royal Academy of Arts,
1933, no. 765, p. 163; K. T. Parker and J. Mathey, *Catalogue
de l'Oeuvre Dessiné d'Antoine Watteau,* Paris: F. de Nobele,
1957, vol. II, no. 577, p. 312, repr. pl. 577; *The Irma N. Straus
Collection of Old Master Drawings,* New York: Parke-Bernet
Galleries, Inc., Oct. 21, 1970, no. 21, repr. in color p. 37

Watteau had a predilection for a feminine type which
appears in nearly all of his drawings of girls and
women. The face was a full oval, the nose slightly
retroussé with large nostrils, the eyes heavy-lidded,
long-lashed, oval shaped, almost slanted, the lips full,
the chin plump, and the hair generally drawn up tightly
into a knot on the top of the head. In the Hammer
portrait—a study which has not been related to a

painting—this easily recognized type appears. The modesty and restraint of the model's pose imply that she was drawn from life, a strong likelihood since it is well-known that Watteau made hundreds of figure studies which he kept in bound volumes and drew upon as elements for his pictures.

This elegantly dressed young lady looks down, but whether in reverie or shyness it is difficult to determine. Watteau has drawn her face in red chalk, touching her eyebrows lightly with black. The red chalk has taken on the grain of the paper, giving it a porous quality. The hair is only briefly indicated by delicate lines, the paper itself left to convey it. Certain of the deep red accents, such as those on the bow of the necklace and on the lips, suggest that the chalk was moistened. Heavy black shading sets the figure off at the right. Despite her youth, the girl, whom the artist has represented with great sympathy, has an expression of maturity.

Watteau's great friend, Comtre de Caylus, has been credited by Seymour de Ricci with having engraved the girl's head in his *Figures de différentes caractères,* no. 273. On the other hand, Parker-Mathey and E. Dacier attribute the engraving to Laurent Cars.

70 Antoine WATTEAU (1684-1721)

Couple Seated on a Bank
Red, black, and white chalk on buff paper
9 1/2″ x 13 3/4″ (24.1 x 34.9 cm.)

Signed lower right in ink: Vataux fecit
Written in crayon lower left: Watteau

Collections: Anonymous Sale (Paris, 1892, no. 72); Lallemand (Sale, Paris, May 2, 1894); Léon Michel-Lévy (Sale, Paris, Galerie Georges Petit, June 17-18, 1925, no. 106); George Blumenthal, New York; Mrs. Jesse I. Straus, New York

Exhibited: Paris, Galerie Georges Petit, *Collection Léon Michel-Lévy,* June 17-18, 1925, no. 106; London, Royal Academy of Arts, *The London Exhibition of French Art, 1200-1900,* Jan. 4-Mar. 12, 1932; no. 738, cat. no. 780 (lent by George Blumenthal); Buffalo, New York, Buffalo Fine Arts Gallery, *Master Drawings...from...Museums and Private Collections of America,* no. 60, pl. 60

Exhibitions: See catalog ref. page
First Exhibited: VII
Not Exhibited: XX, XXIII
Exhibited: Washington, D.C., National Gallery of Art, *National Gallery Exhibition,* June 2-Sept. 1, 1974; Los Angeles, Los Angeles County Museum of Art, *Old Master Drawing Show,* Apr. 29-June 13, 1976

Literature: *Les Maitres du Dessin,* Paris, 1911, vol. III, pl. 136; K. T. Parker, *The Drawings of Antoine Watteau,* London: B. T. Batsford, Ltd., 1931, pl. 92; *Commemorative Catalog of the London Exhibition of French Art, 1200-1900,* London: Royal Academy of Arts, 1933, no. 780, p. 165; K.T. Parker and J. Mathey, *Catalogue de l'Oeuvre Dessiné d'Antoine Watteau,* Paris: F. de Nobele, 1957, no. 665, p. 326, repr. pl. 665; *The Irma N. Straus Collection of Master Drawings,* New York: Parke-Bernet Galleries, Inc., Oct. 21, 1970, no. 20, p. 34

———————————

The great beauty of Watteau's best drawings stems primarily from two factors, the sensitive precision of his line and the enchanting coloristic effects created by his use of three crayons, black red, and white. These features are brilliantly embodied in this sheet. Although the preliminary figures are not shown in the positions they hold in the paintings for which they served, the artist has drawn them in a remarkable way. The arms of the young man serve as an arc to support the figure of the girl; the index finger of his left hand points directly to the nape of her neck; and the right hands of both figures rest parallel to each other on the ground. The juxtaposition of unrelated yet harmoniously arranged figures gives this drawing a fresh, spontaneous character. In contrast to the extreme foreshortening of the man and the sketchiness of his delineation is the complete, detailed rendering of the girl, which adds to the visual impact of the work.

Although Watteau was never in Italy, he is known to have studied the work of Paolo Veronese in Paris. A measure of the elegance, and indeed the fineness of the features of his faces, is undoubtedly derived from the great Venetian master.

The graceful gentleman in the Hammer study appears in at least two Watteau paintings: *La Famille,* in the Rothschild Collection engraved by Aveline (Dacier-Vuaflart, *Jean de Julienne et les graveurs de Watteau...,* III, 1922, no. 86); and *Assemblée Galante* (Dacier-Vuaflart 139).

The sitters in *La Famille* have been identified, on the basis of a document of 1777, as members of the family of Jean Le Bouc-Santussan, a master goldsmith who married the daughter of the famed art dealer, E. P. Gersaint, with whom Watteau lodged for a while.

The *Assemblée Galante* belonged to a French countess who was the mistress of the Duke of Savoy for several years before she returned to Paris where she became the leader of a salon frequented by many great *amateurs* of Watteau. The *Assemblée Galante* was one of two major Watteaus in her sale of 1737, which took place a year after her death.

71 Giovanni Battista TIEPOLO (1696-1770)

St. Jerome in the Desert Listening to the Angels
Pen and brown ink, brown wash, heightened with white,
over black chalk on buff paper: 16 3/4″ x 10 7/8″ (42.5 x
27.6 cm.)

Collections: Formerly in the collection of the Venetian
engraver, Pietro Monaco (1707-1772), engraved and published
by him in 1743 in his *Raccolta di Centododici Stampe di
Pitture della Storia Sacra,* and then re-issued with additional
plates in 1763; Ann Payne Robertson (on loan to The
Metropolitan Museum of Art)

Exhibitions: See catalog ref. page
First Exhibited: VIII
Not Exhibited: X, XX, XXIII
Exhibited: Washington, D.C., National Gallery of Art, on
exhibition, Sept. 21-Nov. 24, 1974; Fort Worth, Texas,
Kimbell Art Museum, on exhibition, Dec. 7, 1974-Feb. 9,
1975; Toledo, Ohio, The Toledo Museum of Art, on
exhibition, Feb. 22-Apr. 20, 1975; Washington, D.C., National
Gallery of Art, *National Gallery Exhibition,* Sept. 21-
Nov. 24, 1975; Los Angeles, California, Los Angeles County
Museum of Art, *Old Master Drawing Show,* Apr. 29-
June 13, 1976

Literature: Sale catalog, *Important Old Master Drawings,*
London: Sotheby & Co., Nov. 26, 1970, no. 71, p. 113,
repr. opp.

This splendid work by Tiepolo belongs to a group of
very finished drawings which the artist probably intended
for sale. Other drawings of a similar type are in the
Museo Civico, Bassano; Museo Civico de Storia ed Arte,
Trieste; the Art Institute of Chicago; the Cleveland
Museum of Art; the Kunstinstitut, Frankfurt; and the
Royal Museum of Fine Arts, Copenhagen.

These drawings have been placed chronologically in
the 1730's and were surely executed by the end of the
decade since they were engraved by Pietro Monaco in
1740. Drawn in pen and rich brown washes, the
drawings are heightened with white, a feature which
Max Goering attributes to the influence upon Tiepolo
by the French artist Louis Dorigny (1654-1742), who
worked for many years in Venice and died in Verona.

72 Giovanni Battista TIEPOLO (1696-1770)

Virgin and Child Adored by Bishops, Monks, and Women
Pen and bister wash over the black chalk on white paper
16 3/4″ x 11 13/16″ (42.5 x 30.0 cm.)

Collections: Prince Alexis Orloff (Sale, Paris, Galerie
Georges Petit, Apr. 29-30, 1920, no. 134); W.W. Crocker,
Burlingame, California; Augustus Pollack, Monterey,
California; R. M. Light & Co., Inc., Boston

Exhibited: San Francisco, California, San Francisco Museum
of Art, *The Opening Exhibition,* Jan.-Mar. 1935; Chicago,
Illinois, Art Institute of Chicago, *Loan Exhibition of
Paintings, Drawings and Prints by the Two Tiepolos:
Giambattista and Giandomenico,* Feb. 4-Mar. 6, 1938, no. 47;
Cambridge, Massachusetts, Harvard University, Fogg Museum
of Art, *Seventy Master Drawings,* Nov. 27, 1948-Jan. 6, 1949,
no. 46

Exhibitions: See catalog ref. page
First Exhibited: XI
Not Exhibited: XX, XXIII
Exhibited: Washington, D.C., National Gallery of Art, on
exhibition, June 2-Sept. 1, 1974

Literature: Otto Benesch, *Venetian Drawings of the 18th
Century in America,* New York: H. Bittner & Co., 1947, no.
19, p. 31, pl. 19; Agnes Mongan, *One Hundred Master
Drawings,* Cambridge: Harvard University Press, 1949, p.
106, repr. opp.; George Knox, "The Orloff Album of Tiepolo
Drawings," *The Burlington Magazine,* London, June 1961,
vol. CIII, no. 15, p. 275

The subject of this drawing is not yet fully identified
although the Virgin is obviously showing favor,
recommending, or interceding for the kneeling male
figure at the left. The loose long hair and seemingly
unclerical attire of this figure do not readily suggest a
relationship to a religious order or with a familiar
saint. The object which he holds in his left hand may
be a small book.

The drawing comes from the well-known *Orloff
Album* which was sold in Paris in 1920. According to
Knox, the album had been assembled by a Russian
dilettante, Gregory Vladimirovitch Orloff (1777-1826),
who published a book on Italian painting. Later the
collection was inherited by Prince Alexis Orloff. The
ninety-six leaves from the album included several which
were highly finished and were often referred to as
presentation drawings.

Benesch and Agnes Mongan have ascribed the
drawing to Tiepolo's mature period since it is looser in
treatment than the preceding work (*Saint Jerome in the
Desert*), but the dark wash which serves to accentuate
the forms is still distributed in the same highly
pictorial manner as in the earlier work. The contouring
by means of a firm continuous line, characteristic of
the earlier style, gives way here to the broken,
accented strokes and modeling by flat washes which
herald the increasingly fugitive means which the artist
adopted in his later drawings.

In the Hammer work the figure of Saint John can be compared generally to the larger figure of Saint Sebastian in the Fogg Museum's drawing entitled *The Holy Family Enthroned with Saints Sebastian, Catherine of Alexandria and Francis,* dated by Knox about 1735. Based on this comparison, the Hammer drawing can probably be assigned the same date rather than Benesch's suggested date of about 1740.

73 François BOUCHER (1703-1770)

Landscape with a Rustic Bridge, ca. 1740
Black chalk, heightened with white on buff paper
8″ x 10 3/4″ (20.3 x 27.3 cm.)

Collections: Fernand Javel, Paris; Charles E. Slatkin Galleries, Inc., New York; Norton Simon, Los Angeles

Exhibitions: See catalog ref. page
First Exhibited: IX
Not Exhibited: XX, XXIII

Literature: *Great Drawings of All Time, French: 13th Century to 1919* (selected and edited by Ira Moskowitz, text by Agnes Mongan), New York: Shorewood Publishers, Inc., 1962, vol. III, no. 696, repr. opp.; Sale catalog, *Property of the Norton Simon Foundation and Old Master Drawings and Paintings, from the Private Collection of Norton Simon,* New York; Parke-Bernet Galleries, Inc., May 7, 1971, no. 207, p. 160, repr. opp.

––––––––––––

Fully published by Agnes Mongan in *Great Drawings of All Time* (Shorewood, 1962, vol. III, no. 696), this drawing is assigned to the period of 1740 when Boucher, then designing for tapestries, made frequent trips into the country en route to Beauvais and the Gobelins.

It is noteworthy that in his own time Boucher was roundly criticized by the Revolution for his pastoral paintings; his countryside was considered romantic and his peasants disguised aristocrats. But a truer note came out in his landscape drawings. Here Boucher took his cue from such Dutch masters as Jacob Ruisdael and Jan van Goyen who were among the artists whose work he collected and studied. In consequence, his landscape drawings have a tranquility and restraint which contrast with the energetic sensuousness of his figural works. On the whole, the figures in his landscape drawings are subordinated to the setting, sometimes, as in the present work, appearing as staffage.

Boucher is known to have formed his drawing style upon that of Watteau whom he copied and engraved. It

was this influence which led him to develop his supple contouring and expressive accenting of light and dark. However, the thirty years that separated the two artists can be detected in the change from the older artist's straight, uninterrupted line to the undulant, rococo forms of the younger man. But Boucher's landscape drawings were still marked by a firm lineality in which short flecks of the crayon delineated the foliage and lead white was added to create the shimmer of light in the distance.

74 François BOUCHER (1703-1770)

Venus Reclining against a Dolphin
Black chalk heightened with white
9″ x 13 1/2″ (22.8 x 34.3 cm.)

Collections: Charles E. Slatkin Galleries, Inc., New York; Norton Simon, Los Angeles

Exhibitions: See catalog ref. page
First Exhibited: IX
Not Exhibited: XX, XXIII

Exhibited: Washington, D.C., National Gallery of Art, *Drawings by François Boucher,* Dec. 25, 1973-Mar. 15, 1974; Chicago, Illinois, The Art Institute of Chicago, *Drawings by François Boucher,* Apr. 1, 1974-May 20, 1974

Literature: Marcel Roux, *Inventaire du Fonds Français, Graveurs du XVIIIème Siècle,* Paris: Bibliothèque Nationale, Département des Estampes, 1949, vol. IV, no. 88, p. 367; Alexandre Aranoff, *L'Oeuvre Dessiné de François Boucher,* Catalogue Raisonné, Paris: F. de Nobele, vol. 1, no. 801A p. 208 (counterproof), (engraved by Demarteau); Sale catalog, *Property of the Norton Simon Foundation and Old Master Drawings and Paintings, from the Private Collection of Norton Simon,* New York: Parke-Bernet Galleries, Inc., May 7, 1971, no. 206, p. 158, repr. opp.

––––––––––––

Among the artists of the Rococo, Boucher was the leading reviver of mythological subjects and the interpreter of the female nude who endowed it with the greatest of voluptuousness. The obvious sensuousness of his nudes contrasts, for example, with the non-sensual, classically influenced nudes of Rubens.

Boucher executed about fifty drawings on the theme of Venus, "the divinity adored by the Courtiers of the age of Louis XV." Several studies by Boucher show the goddess in a reclining position, similar to that of the present work, but with different attributes. The Hammer drawing is a rare Boucher counterproof, reinforced by the artist. The location of its counterpart is not known at present.

In Boucher's time counterproofs were made when the chalk medium was still quite fresh and susceptible to transfer. This was done by means of skillful rubbing after the backs of both the first drawing and of the blank sheet were moistened to assist in the process. The artist could then rework the transferred impression and have the reversed composition as another "original" after his first original drawing. This method was also practiced by Fragonard who was compelled by the great demand for his drawings to use this quasi-print technique. Boucher, on the other hand, had students make replicas of his drawings, and counterproofs are not frequent in his work. In the Eighteenth Century many collectors preferred counterproofs because they were more "delicate" in tone than the designs from which they were pressed. Unlike prints, however, a counterproof, like a monotype, did not yield more than one acceptable impression.

75   Jean-Baptiste GREUZE (1725-1805)

A Tired Mother with Two Children
Pen and brown ink over black lead, 9″ x 11″ (22.5 x 27.8 cm.)

Exhibitions: Not previously exhibited

76   Jean-Honoré FRAGONARD (1732-1806)

Study for the Education of the Virgin
Charcoal: 10 15/16″ x 8 9/16″ (27.8 x 21.7 cm.)

Collections: Private Collection, France; Private Collection, New York; Wildenstein and Co., New York

Exhibitions: See catalog ref. page
First Exhibited: XXXII

Literature: *The Sentinal Rome,* New York, November 23, 1960, ill.

————————————

This drawing bears compositional and stylistic similarities to three paintings catalogued by George Wildenstein in his book *The Paintings of Fragonard* published in 1960 (see: #17, Fig. 11, #18, Plate 1, #19, Plate 2).

77   Jean-Honoré FRAGONARD (1732-1806)

The Reading
Brown wash, the corners rounded out:
11″ x 8 1/4″ (27.9 x 21.0 cm.)

Collections: H. Walferdin (Sale, Paris, Apr. 12-16, 1880, no. 192); J. P. Heseltine, London; E. H. Molyneux, Neuilly-sur-Seine; Mrs. Jesse I. Straus, New York (Sale, New York, Parke-Bernet Galleries, Inc., Oct. 21, 1970, no. 32)

Exhibited: London, *National Loan Exhibition,* 1909-1910, no. 99; New York: E. Gimpel and Wildenstein & Co., Inc., *Paintings and Drawings by Fragonard,* Jan. 1914, no. 31; Paris, Musée Carnavalet, *La Vie Parisienne au XVIIIème Siècle,* Mar. 20-Apr. 30, 1928, no. 165; Paris, Jacques Seligmann et Fils, Ancien Hôtel de Sagan, *Exposition de Dessins de Fragonard, Pour la Maison Santé du Gardien de la Paix,* May 9-30, 1931, no. 55 (lent by E. H. Molyneux)

Exhibitions: See catalog ref. page
First Exhibited: VII
Not Exhibited: X, XX, XXIII

Literature: Baron Roger Portalis, *Fragonard, Sa Vie et Son Oeuvre,* Paris: J. Rothschild, 1889, p. 307; *Drawings by François Boucher, J.-H. Fragonard and Antoine Watteau in the Collection of J. P. H. (Heseltine),* London: The Autotype Company, 1900, no. 4, p. 39 (the engraving by Jules de Goncourt was reproduced in place of the drawing); *Dessins de l'Ecole Française du XVIIIéme Siècle, Provenant de la Collection Heseltine,* Paris: Frazier-Soye, 1913, no. 32, repr.; *Catalogue of Paintings and Drawings by Fragonard,* New York: Gimpel and Wildenstein & Co., Inc., 1914, no. 31, p. 54; Alexandre Ananoff, L'Oeuvre Dessiné de J.-H. Fragonard, *Catalogue Raisonné,* Paris: F. de Nobele, 1961, vol. I, no. 62, p. 55, fig. 28; Sale catalog, *The Irma N. Straus Collection of Old Master Drawings,* New York: Parke-Bernet Galleries, Inc., Oct. 21, 1970, no. 32, p. 58, repr. opp.

————————————

Traditionally this drawing has been held to represent Madame Fragonard reading to her younger sister, Marguerite Gerard, who came to live with the Fragonards after their marriage and was not only the pupil of the artist, but one of his favorite models. Both women were accomplished miniaturists, and Marguerite left a fine small portrait in oil of her celebrated brother-in-law.

Like the *Visit to the Nurse,* this drawing was originally in the H. Walferdin Collection which was formed in Paris during Fragonard's lifetime. Walferdin (1795-1880) was born in the same city as Diderot and shared his admiration for Fragonard. Physician and occasional man of politics, Walferdin's true pursuits were literature and art, and he was able to acquire an exceptional group of drawings by his favorite artist.

Themes centering around letters, or the exchange of confidences, and similar *tête-a-tête* situations were popular with Fragonard's audience because they implied human drama or romance. But quieter scenes of familial intimacy were rarer in his work. *The Reading* records such a mood of quiet intimacy. The two sisters sit together, one reading to the other. The younger, drawn in profile, occupies the foreground with the volume of her full skirt, and the older is seen from the rear. The heads of the two women incline towards each other as they share a mutual involvement in the book.

The whole drawing is suffused and unified by the golden tonality of the paper. The dainty, elegant silhouette of Marguerite ranks with the happiest of Fragonard's figures in which the essential is conveyed through a minimum of details. The figures of both women are, in fact, treated more broadly here than in the identical wash drawing in the Louvre (Ananoff 61).

78   Jean-Honoré FRAGONARD (1732-1806)

Grandfather's Reprimand
Gray-brown wash over black chalk
13 1/2" x 17 3/4" (34.3 x 45.1 cm.)

Collections: Louis-Antoine-August Rohan-Chabot (Sale, Paris, Dec. 8, 1807, no. 43); Baron Vivant-Denon (Sale, Paris, May 1-19, 1826, no. 732); Baron Brunet-Denon (Sale, Paris, Feb. 2, 1846, no. 269); H. Walferdin (Sale, Paris, Apr. 12-16, 1880, no. 199); Comte de Jaucourt, Paris; Sigismond Bardas, Paris; Georges and Florence Blumenthal (Sale, Paris, Dec. 1-2, 1932, no. 30); Jacques Seligmann, Paris; Mrs. Jesse I. Straus, New York (Sale, New York, Parke-Bernet Galleries, Inc., Oct. 21, 1970, no. 34)

Exhibited: Paris, Musée des Arts Décoratifs, Pavillon de Marsan, Palais du Louvre, *Exposition d'Oeuvres de J.-H. Fragonard,* June 7-July 10, 1921, no. 133

Exhibitions: See catalog ref. page
First Exhibited: VII
Not Exhibited: XX, XXIII

Literature: *Catalogue of the Sale of Baron Vivant-Denon,* Paris: Imprimerie d'Hippolyte Tilliard, 1826, no. 732, p. 178; Baron Roger Portalis, *Honoré Fragonard, Sa Vie et Son*

Oeuvre, Paris: J. Rothschild, 1889, p. 311; Georges Wildenstein, *Catalogue de l'Exposition d'Oeuvres de J.-H. Fragonard,* Musée des Arts Décoratifs, Paris: Frazier-Soye, 1921, no. 133; *Catalogue of the Sale of the Georges and Florence Blumenthal Collection,* Paris: Galerie Georges Petit, 1932, no. 30, p. 28, repr. pl. 10, Louis Réau, *Fragonard, Sa Vie et Son Oeuvre,* Brussels: Elsevier, 1956, p. 206; Alexandre Ananoff, *L'Oeuvre Dessiné de J.-H. Fragonard, Catalogue Raisonné,* Paris: F. de Nobele, 1961, no. 41, p. 46; Sale catalog, *The Irma N. Straus Collection of Master Drawings,* New York: Parke-Bernet Galleries, Inc., Oct. 21, 1970, no. 34, p. 62, repr. opp.

Portalis indicates that this drawing has had various titles in the course of time: *La Prière, au grand-père,* 1846; *La Prière,* 1880; *La Réprimande du grund-papa,* 1889; and *La Visite chez le docteur,* 1921-1932, according to Georges Wildenstein.

Although chalk was the primary drawing medium of Watteau and Boucher, Fragonard, influenced by Tiepolo, revived the technique of drawing with ink and wash. When he visited Italy as a young man, Fragonard was overpowered by Michelanglo and Raphael but was able to make copies of what he in his own words called "second-raters like Pietro da Cortona and Giovanni Battista Tiepolo."

Of the four Hammer Fragonards the most splendid must be considered these two drawings of children for which the artist's young son, Alexandre-Evariste, called Fanfan, is believed to have been the inspiration. Fragonard married comparatively late, at the age of thirty-seven, and had two children with his eighteen-year-old bride from his native city of Grasse, in Provence. In these two delicious interludes, *The Little Preacher* and *Grandfather's Reprimand,* the great French artist of *l'amour,* the brilliant portrayer of the frivolous pursuit, turned to familial themes with the same immediacy and verve which made his work so delightful to the Paris of his youth.

The outstanding features of these two drawings are the broad, flowing brushstrokes of the darker wash and the light which floods the compositions with a vibrating, dissolving intensity. Totally suffused and illuminated, the figures themselves, despite their vigorous, broad execution and volume, seem painted with the same airiness as the palpitating atmosphere which surrounds them. Both were loose and free. Fragonard's works were much like his contemporary, Tiepolo, in terms of their graphic techniques. While Tiepolo still remained tied to the tradition of the line, Fragonard, on the other hand, "painted" drawings such as these over nebulous preliminary black chalk indications.

79 Jean-Honoré FRAGONARD (1732-1806)

The Little Preacher
Brown wash over black chalk
13 3/4″ x 18 1/4″ (34.9 x 46.7 cm.)

Collections: Anonymous Sale (Paris, May 31, 1790, no. 180); M. Marmontel (Sale, Paris, Hôtel Drouot, Jan. 25-26, 1883, no. 100); Richard Lion (Sale, Paris, Hôtel Drouot, Apr. 3, 1886, no. 40); M.P. Ledoux (Sale, Paris, Galerie Georges Petit, Mar. 5, 1918, no. 27); Adrien Fauchier-Magnan, Neuilly-sur-Seine; Arthur Veil-Picard, Paris; Guiraud Brothers, Paris; Mrs. Jesse I. Straus, New York

Exhibitions: See catalog ref. page
First Exhibited: VII
Not Exhibited: XX, XXIII

Literature: Baron Roger Portalis, *Honoré Fragonard, Sa Vie et Son Oeuvre*, Paris; J. Rothschild, 1889, pp. 200, 310; Edmond and Jules de Goncourt, *L'Art du XVIIIème Siècle—Fragonard*, Paris: Edition 1914, pp. 300-301; *Catalogue des Tableaux Anciens et Modernes, Aquarelles et Dessins de la Vente M. P. Ledoux*, Paris: Galerie Georges Petit, 1918, no. 27, p. 20: *Connaissance des Arts*, Aug. 1956, repr., p. 42; Louis Réau, *Fragonard, Sa Vie et Son Oeuvre*, Brussels: Elsevier, 1956, p. 205, fig. 79, p. 82; Alexandre Ananoff, *L'Oeuvre Dessiné de J.-H. Fragonard, Catalogue Raisonné*, Paris: F. de Nobele, 1961, vol. I, no. 40, p. 45, fig. 18; Sale catalog, *The Irma N. Straus Collection of Old Master Drawings*, New York; Parke-Bernet Galleries, Inc., Oct. 21, 1970, no. 31, p. 56, repr. opp.

———————————

Ananoff describes *The Little Preacher* as Fanfan, the son of Fragonard. Engraved with variations by N. de Launay in 1781 as a pendant to *L 'Education Fait Tout*, now in the collection of Baron E. de Rothschild (Ananoff, no. 11, fig. 6). This engraving may have been made from the painting of the same subject formerly in the Veil-Picard Collection (Wildenstein, no. 471).

80 Jean-Honoré FRAGONARD (1732-1806)

Visit to the Nurse
Chinese ink wash, heightened with watercolor
12″ x 15″ (30.5 x 38.1 cm.)

Collections: Frédéric Villot (Sale, Paris, Hôtel Drouot, May 16-18, 1859, no. 122); E. H. Molyneux, Neuilly-sur-Seine; H. Walferdin (Sale, Paris, Apr. 12-16, 1880, no. 200); Prince A. d'Arenberg, Paris; Jacques Seligmann, Paris; Mrs. Jesse I. Straus, New York

Exhibited: Berlin, Académie Royale des Arts, *Exposition d'Oeuvres de l'Art Français au XVIIIème Siècle*, Jan.-Mar. 1910, no. 178; Paris, Musée Carnavalet, *La Vie Parisienne au XVIIIème Siècle*, Mar. 20-Apr. 30, 1928, no. 166; Paris, Galerie Jacques Seligmann et Fils, Ancien Hôtel de Sagan, *Exposition de Dessins de Fragonard, Pour la Maison Santé au Gardien de la Paix*, May 9-30, 1931, no. 22

Exhibitions: See catalog ref. page
First Exhibited: VII
Not Exhibited: X, XX, XXIII

Literature: Sale catalog, *Catalogue de la Vente M.F. Villot, Dessins, Miniatures et Estampes*, Paris: Hôtel Drouot, 1859, no. 122; p. 20; Académie Royale des Arts, *Catalogue de l'Exposition d'Oeuvres de l'Art Français au XVIIIème Siècle*, Berlin: La Société Photographiques, 1910, no. 178, p. 41; Louis Réau, *Fragonard, Sa Vie et Son Oeuvre*, Brussels: Elsevier, 1956, pp. 81, 206; Sale catalog, *The Irma N. Straus Collection of Old Master Drawings*, New York: Parke-Bernet Galleries, Inc., Oct. 21, 1970, no. 30, p. 54, repr. opp.

———————————

Fragonard frequently depicted the same subject in a drawing as well as in a painting. In some instances the drawings were studies for the later painted work; for example, preparatory drawings are known for the *Education of the Virgin*, the oil on panel now in the Hammer Collection.

Portalis (p. 291) lists a painting, the subject of which, like the Hammer drawing of the *Visit to the Nurse*, was taken from *Miss Sara*, an English novel which had been translated into French. The *Visit to the Nurse* portrays the theme of parental affection and pride. The treatment of the subject almost suggests, or parallels, an Adoration of the Child in religious art. All the figures are assembled on the foreground plane, with the light from the upper left trained on the *paterfamilias* who holds his infant. The graded layers of the gray washes throw the illuminated figures into brilliant relief, as though the scene were taking place on a stage.

Presenting a polar contrast to his celebrated works on the theme of love, the familial themes in Fragonard's oeuvre reflected Eighteenth-Century French society's pleasure in intimate home-life episodes. Such episodes were most popularly portrayed in the work of Fragonard's contemporary, J. B. Greuze. But while the latter, strongly reflecting the ideas of Rousseau and

Diderot, frequently infused moralistic and didactic precepts into his art, Fragonard, although partaking of the "sentimentality" of his era, was free of the social propaganda advanced by the revolutionists. As is well known, Fragonard did not fit into the new order after the French Revolution. Rather, he quickly declined in status, eventually dying in poverty and obscurity in his native city of Grasse.

81   Jean-Auguste-Dominique INGRES (1780-1867)

Mrs. Badham
Pencil on white wove paper
10 1/4″ x 8 1/4″ (26.0 x 21.0 cm.)
Signed and dated lower left: J. Ingres, Del Roma 1816

Collections: Charles Badham (d. 1845); The Badham Family; C. Badham Jackson (Sale, London, Sotheby & Co., Inc., Dec. 12, 1928, no. 145, repr.); Wildenstein & Co., Inc., New York, 1929; Mrs. Jesse I. Straus, New York (Sale, New York, Parke-Bernet Galleries, Inc., Oct. 21, 1970, no. 49, repr.)

Exhibited: New York, Paul Rosenberg Gallery, *Loan Exhibition of Ingres in American Collections,* Apr. 7-May 6, 1961, no. 22, p. 32, repr.; Cambridge, Massachusetts, Fogg Art Museum, Harvard University, *Ingres Centennial Exhibition, 1867-1967, Drawings, Watercolors and Oil Sketches from American Collections,* Feb. 12-Apr. 9, 1967, no. 37, repr.; International Exhibitions Foundation: *Ingres in Rome,* Washington, D.C., National Gallery of Art, Jan. 23-Feb. 21, 1971; Philadelphia, Pennsylvania, Philadelphia Museum of Art, Mar. 16-Apr. 11, 1971, New York, Wildenstein & Co., Inc., Apr. 24-May 23, 1971; Washington, D.C., National Gallery of Art, on exhibition, June 2-Sept. 1, 1974; Washington, D.C., National Gallery of Art, *Ingres in Rome,* Jan. 23-Feb. 21, 1971; Philadelphia, Pennsylvania, Philadelphia, Museum of Art, *Ingres in Rome,* Mar. 16-Apr. 11, 1971; New York, New York, Wildenstein Gallery, *Ingres in Rome,* Apr. 24-May 23, 1971

Exhibitions: See catalog ref. page
First Exhibited: VII
Not Exhibited: X
Exhibited: Washington, D.C., National Gallery of Art, on exhibition, June 2-Sept. 1, 1974

Literature: Morton D. Zabel, "Ingres in America," *The Arts,* Feb. 1930, vol. XVI, no. 6, p. 378, repr.; Jean Cassou, "Ingres et Ses Contradictions," *Gazette des Beaux-Arts,* vol. XI, Mar. 1934, p. 157, fig. 15, Brinsley Ford, "Ingres Portrait Drawings of English People at Rome, 1806-1820," *The Burlington Magazine,* vol. LXXV, July 1939, no. 436, p. 8 ff., pl. IIIC; Hans Naef, *Rome Vue par Ingres,* Lausanne: Le Guide du Livre, 1960, p. 27, fig. 52; *Apollo,* Oct. 1970, 92:128, repr.; *Apollo,* Jan. 1971, 93:78, repr.; Sale catalog

The Irma N. Straus Collection of Old Master Drawings, New York: Parke-Bernet Galleries, Inc., Oct. 21, 1970, no. 49, p. 92, repr. opp.

This drawing ranks among the most enchanting made by Ingres of English visitors to Rome in the second decade of the Nineteenth Century. He did fewer drawings of Englishmen than of his own countrymen, but they belong to the most outstanding of his pencil portraits as exemplified, for instance, by the Los Angeles Museum's *Portrait of Thomas Church,* executed in 1816, the same year as this drawing.

In addition to her beauty, Mrs. Badham has always had a special claim to fame as the first cousin of the noted English poet, Thomas Campbell (1777-1844), author of many patriotic lyrics and related verse.

As in the Fogg Museum's double portrait of *Mrs. Vesey and her Daughter* (Mongan-Naef, no. 36), Ingres here obviously took great delight in the details of his subject's attire, from the frills of her bonnet to her conspicuously draped Roman-striped scarf. All of these details are drawn with blunt and shaded strokes which heighten the contrast with the extremely delicate stippling of the soft face and long, slender neck, a contrast further emphasized by the dark accents of the profuse curls. In depicting all of these decorations of Mrs. Badham's person, Ingres has drawn a beguiling image of the charming feminine overdress of the early Nineteenth Century.

In addition to the fascinating appeal of the sitter, the off-center contraposto position she occupies further heightens the visual interest of the composition. The artist placed her so as to provide a view of the Villa Medici and the obelisk at the top of Spanish Steps in the background.

Mrs. Badham and her family and Ingres lived near each other on the Via Gregoriana, the same street as that portrayed here.

82   Honoré DAUMIER (1808-1879)

Third Class Carriage
Red chalk on blue paper:
10 9/16″ x 13″ (26.7 x 33.0 cm.)
Unsigned

Collections: Roger Marx, Paris; Strolin, Paris; Hirshland, New York; Myrtil Frank, New York

Exhibitions: See catalog ref. page
First Exhibited: XXXII

Literature: Catalogue de la Vente Roger Marx, Paris 1914, II no. 108; Erich Klossowski *Honoré Daumier,* Munich 1923, no. 258C; K. E. Maison *Honoré Daumier—Catalogue Raisonné*, vol. II, no. 287, ill. pl. 74

———————

Note: This drawing is very close (in reverse) to the painting I-178 in Maison; the painting, however, shows the traveler's hand resting on his knees.

83   Honoré DAUMIER (1808-1879)

The Pleading Lawyer
Watercolor, ink, and gouache: 6 1/4″ x 8 1/2″ (15.9 x 21.6 cm.)

Collections: Bellino (Sale, Paris, 1892, no. 32); H. P. (Sale, Paris, 1901, no. 5); Paul Gallimard, Paris; Paul Cassirer, Berlin; Jakob Goldschmidt, Berlin and New York; Alfred E. Goldschmidt, Stamford, Conn.

Exhibited: Paris, Palais du Louvre, *Exposition de Tableaux, Statues et Objets d'Arts, au Profit de l'Oeuvre des Orphelins d'Alsace Lorraine*, 1885, no. 101 (lent by Bellino); Paris Ecole des Beaux-Arts, *Exposition des Peintures, Aquarelles, Dessins et Lithographies des Maîtres de la Caricature, et de la Peinture de Moeurs au XIXème Siècle*, 1888, no. 392; Paris, Exposition Universelle, *Exposition Centennale de l'Art Français*, 1889, no. 135 (lent by Bellino); Paris, Galerie L. and P. Rosenberg, *Exposition de Dessins, Aquarelles et Lithographies de Honoré Daumier*, Apr. 15-May 6, 1907 (lent by Gallimard); St. Petersbourg, *L'Art Français, Exposition Centennale*, Jan. 15-28, 1912, no. 3 (lent by Jakob Goldschmidt); Berlin, Galerie Paul Cassirer, *Ein Jahrhundert Französischer Zeichnung*, Dec. 1929-Jan. 1930, no. 17; London, Matthiesen Gallery, *A Century of French Drawings*, May 3-21, 1938, no. 39; London, Tate Gallery, The Arts Council of Great Britain, *Daumier—Paintings and Drawings*, June 14-July 30, 1961, no. 223 (lent by Mr. and Mrs. A. E. Goldschmidt)

Exhibitions: See catalog ref. page
First Exhibited: VII
Not Exhibited: XXIII

Literature: Ecole des Beaux-Arts, *Catalogue de l'Exposition des Peintures, Aquarelles, Dessins et Lithographies des Maîtres Français de la Caricature*, Paris: Maison Quantin, 1888 (Préface Paul Mantz), *(Gazette des Beaux-Arts)*, no. 392, p. 85; Armand Dayot, *Un Siècle d'Art, Notes sur la Peinture Française à l'Exposition Centennale des Beaux-Arts, Catalogue Complet des Oeuvres Exposées*, Paris: Librairie Plon, 1890, p. 150; René Jean, *Catalogue Commemoratif, L'Art Français à Saint-Petersbourg, Exposition Centennale*, Paris: Goupil et Cie, Manzi-Joyant et Cie, 1912, no. 3, p. 34; Erich Klossowski, *Honoré Daumier*, Munich: R. Piper Co., 1923, no. 177b, p. 102; Eduard Fuchs, *Der Maler Daumier*, New York: E. Weyhe, Leipzig: Hesse & Backet, 1927, and

1930, no. 198a, p. 54, repr. pl. 198; K. E. Maison, *Daumier Drawings*, New York and London: Thomas Yoseloff, 1960, no. 134, p. 29, repr. pl. 134; Arts Council of Great Britain, *Catalogue of an Exhibition of Daumier Paintings and Drawings at the Tate Gallery*, London: Curwen Press, 1961, no. 223, p. 67; K. E. Maison, *Honoré Daumier, Catalogue Raisonné of the Paintings, Watercolours and Drawings*, England and The Netherlands: New York Graphic Society, Ltd., 1968, vol. II, no. 675, repr. pl. 259; Sale catalog, *Important Impressionist and Modern Paintings and Drawings*, New York: Parke-Bernet Galleries, Inc., Oct. 28, 1970, no. 13, p. 24, repr. opp.

———————

The legal profession was one which allowed Daumier the full vent of his piercing satire. He scarcely made a study of that occupation which did not expose its hypocrisy, rapacity, and stentorian oratory. At the same time, these devastating interpretations were cushioned by the artist's overriding comic sense with the result that lawyers and judges became objects of laughter rather than of derision and scorn.

The Hammer watercolor is a rare example of a Daumier interpretation of a lawyer, in that it is not risible but, on the contrary, almost sympathetic. The subject is an old, buck-toothed pleader who is shown in an intense, impassioned moment which seems to embody a lifetime of courtroom behavior and to capture the timelessness of ingrained custom. Light illuminates the intent, even earnest, wrinkled face, its expression molded by constant harangue, silhouettes the semaphoric right hand, and falls sensitively on the knuckles of the other in which the brief is clasped. The head, so intensely realistic that one can almost hear the lawyer's words, is drawn with Daumier's unique lineality, composed of s-curves, arcs, parentheses, and other generally serpentine strophes, deftly but economically applied. The scene is completed with watercolor, the robes and hat heightened with gouache. Daumier fully signed the work which, although relatively small, is a highly finished masterpiece among his legal subjects.

The difficulty of arriving at an exact chronology for many of Daumier's drawings and watercolors has been pointed out repeatedly. K. E. Maison suggested that the time span between "early" and "late" works in Daumier's oeuvre may be as much as twenty-five years. A systematic or consistent evolution in the artist's drawings appears improbable, and his studies and sketches defy definite dating.

Although the Hammer drawing has not been dated by Maison, a reasonable or justifiable chronology for Daumier's large group of drawings of legal subjects may be suggested by their apparent relationship to the thirty-nine lithographs, *Le Gens de Justice*, which were printed in *Le Charivari* from 1845 to 1848. Jean

Adhémar has placed many paintings, drawings, and watercolors of legal subjects in the period of 1843-1846 although he dates a spirited drawing. *Lawyer*, in the Boymans Museum as late as about 1865. Maison places a drawing, *Les deux avocats*, in 1860.

84 Honoré DAUMIER (1808-1879)

Two Women and a Child
Pen and brown and black wash, heightened with white chalk: 8 1/4″ x 7 1/16″ (21.0 x 18.0 cm.)
Initialled

Exhibited: Paris, Durand-Ruel, 1878, no. 123; Paris, Beaux-Arts, 1901, no. 160

Exhibitions: Not previously exhibited

———————————

It has repeatedly been suggested that this drawing may represent the Virgin holding the Infant Christ, with St. Anne.

85 Jean-François MILLET (1814-1875)

Peasants Resting
Pastel: 16 3/4″ x 20 1/4″ (42.5 x 51.4 cm.)

Collections: Boussod and Valadon, Paris; Leonard Gow, Scotland; Barbizon House, London; L. M. Flesh, Piqua, Ohio, (Sale, London, Sotheby & Co., July 9, 1958, no. 101, p. 21, repr.); Thomas Agnew & Sons, Ltd., London: Norton Simon, Los Angeles (Sale, New York, Parke-Bernet Galleries, Inc., May 5, 1971, no. 23, repr.)

Exhibited: Paris, Ecole des Beaux-Arts, *Exposition Millet*, 1887, no. 96

Exhibitions: See catalog ref. page
First Exhibited: IX
Not Exhibited: X, XXIII

Literature: Ecole des Beaux-Arts, *Catalogue Descriptif des Peintures, Aquarelles, Pastels, Dessins, Rehaussés, Croquis et Eaux-fortes de J. F. Millet, au Profit de la Souscription pour Elever un Monument à la Mémoire du Maître*, Paris: Imprimerie Quantin, 1887, p. 70, no. 96, (by MM. Boussod and Valadon); *An Illustrated Record*, Barbizon House, 1937, no. 41, repr.; Sale catalog, *Highly Important 19th and 20th Century Paintings, Drawings and Sculpture, from the Private Collection of Norton Simon*, New York: Parke-Bernet Galleries, Inc., May 5, 1971, no. 23, p. 38, repr. opp. in color

———————————

The subject is a typical one for Millet—peasants resting from their labors. In this case the man uses a tinderbox to light his pipe, while the woman, seated on

the ground, watches him. Moreau-Nélaton (*Millet raconté par lui-même*, Paris, 1921, vol. 3) reproduces a variant (III, fig. 223) which he dates 1866, and two pencil sketches (III, figs. 341-342) one of which (341) is clearly for this pastel. The work is known in French as *Le Briquet*, the tinderbox.

86 Eugène BOUDIN (1824-1898)

Beach Scene
Pencil and watercolor: 4 5/8″ x 9 7/16″ (11.7 x 24.0 cm.)
Signed and dated lower right: Boudin 69
Inscribed lower left: Trouville

Exhibitions: See catalog ref. page
First Exhibited: II
Not Exhibited: XX, XXIII

———————————

Boudin favored water-color to give transparency to his compositions and to capture the evanescent light effects of the beaches at which he worked. The dark range of figures defining a lateral middleground against a light foreground and background (beach and sky) is typical of him. The horizontal format helps in the diffusion of focus. This scene, like the Hammer *Beach at Trouville*, shows fashionable figures taking their ease at a popular resort.

87 Camille PISSARRO (1830-1903)

Pea Harvest, ca. 1880 (recto)
Watercolor and charcoal: 9″ x 11″ (22.8 x 27.9 cm.)
Signed lower right: C.P.
Portrait of George (verso)
Pencil and watercolor: 8 1/2″ x 11 5/8″ (21.6 x 29.5 cm.)

Collections: M. Knoedler & Co., Inc., New York; Mrs. Henry Gerstle, New York

Exhibitions: See catalog ref. page
First Exhibited: II
Not Exhibited: IX, XX, XXIII

Literature: Sale catalog, *Important Drawings and Watercolors of the 19th and 20th Centuries*, New York: Parke-Bernet Galleries, Inc., May 15, 1969, no. 40A, repr. opp.

88 Camille PISSARRO (1830-1903)

Montmorency Road
Pencil: 9 1/4″ x 12 3/8″ (23.5 x 31.4 cm.)
Estate stamp lower left: C.P.
Inscribed lower right: Montmorency Enghien

Exhibitions: See catalog ref. page
First Exhibited: II
Not Exhibited: X, XX, XXIII

89 Edouard MANET (1832-1883)

Man Wearing a Cloak, 1852-1858 (recto)
Charcoal: 16″ x 8 3/4″ (40.6 x 19.7 cm.)
Signed lower left with initials: ed. m.
Man Wearing a Cloak (verso)
Charcoal: 16″ x 8 3/4″ (40.6 x 19.7 cm.)

Collections: Hector Brown; Arcade Gallery, London; Francis
Cooke, Esq.; Matthiesen Gallery, London; Hugh Chisholm,
New York

Exhibitions: See catalog ref. page
First Exhibited: VI
Not Exhibited: X, XX, XXIII

Literature: Alain de Leiris, *The Drawings of Edouard Manet,*
Berkeley and Los Angeles: University of California Press,
1969, no. 135 (recto) and no. 136 (verso), repr. figs. 186, 187;
Sale catalog, *Impressionist and Modern Drawings, Paintings
and Sculpture,* London: Christie, Manson & Woods, June 30,
1970, no. 1, repr.

These monumental studies of mantled figures were
drawn under the influence of Manet's teacher, Thomas
Couture, who encouraged a broad style of modeling,
with large masses of light, blocked out by straight and
simplified lineal contouring. This approach was based
on the bold technique used by the Italian masters of
the Renaissance in fresco painting. Manet made many
drawings after Renaissance artists in order to master
the elements of design and composition. However, in
the present drawings the glancing surfaces of light
created from the reserved parts of the paper bespeak
Manet's early interest in a flattening and generalizing
of the form rather than in its strict structural volume.

90 Edgar DEGAS (1834-1917)

Jacquet
Pastel: 10 1/4″ x 8 1/8″ (26.0 x 20.6 cm.)
Signed center right: Degas

Collections: Professor Hermann Heilbuth, Copenhagen:
Bachstitz Galleries; Mrs. Jesse I. Straus, New York

Exhibitions: See catalog ref. page
First Exhibited: VII
Not Exhibited: XX, XXIII

Literature: *Art News,* Mar. 7, 1931, p. 5, repr.; Jean Sutherland
Boggs, *Portraits by Degas,* Berkeley and Los Angeles:
University of California Press, 1962, p. 120 (wherein the
drawing is dated ca. 1878); Sale catalog, *The Irma N. Straus
Collection of Old Master Drawings,* New York: Parke-Bernet
Galleries, Inc., Oct. 21, 1970, p. 94, no. 50

Degas was a master at establishing three-dimensional
volume without sacrificing a sense of the surface on
which he was working, in this case the bare paper. Of
the subject of his drawing Jean Sutherland Boggs notes
laconically, "know nothing of him." At the time the work
entered the Straus Collection, however, *Art News*
identified Jacquet as Degas' frame maker. Miss Boggs
dates the portrait 1878.

91 Edgar DEGAS (1834-1917)

Theater Box, 1885
Pastel: 22″ x 16 1/2″ (56.0 x 41.0 cm.)

Collections: Atelier Degas (2nd Sale, Paris, Galerie Georges
Petit, Dec. 11-13, 1918, no. 162, repr.); Mlle. Jeanne Fèvre,
Nice (the artist's niece), (Sale, Paris, June 12, 1934, no. 94);
Mrs. Kay, Berkshire; Reid and Léfèvre Galleries, Glasgow
and London; James Archdale

Exhibitions: See catalog ref. page
First Exhibited: XI
Not Exhibited: XXIII

Literature: Sale catalog, *Catalogue des Tableaux, Pastels et
Dessins par Edgar Degas,* 2nd Sale, Paris: Galerie Georges
Petit, 1918, p. 87, no. 162, repr.; Sale catalog, *Catalogue des
Tableaux, Aquarelles, Pastels, Dessins, Estampes et
Monotypes par Edgar Degas,* Paris: Galerie Jean Charpentier,
1934, no. 94, pl. VII, repr.; P.A. Lemoisne, *Degas et son
Oeuvre,* Paris: Paul Brame and C.M. de Hauke, 1947, vol. III,
p. 480, no. 829, repr.; Lillian Browse, *Degas Dancers,* New
York: The Studio Publications, 1949, p. 347, no. 110, pl. 110
and frontispiece, repr. in color; Sale catalog, *Impressionist
and Modern Drawings, Paintings and Sculpture,* London:
Christie, Manson & Woods, 1971, p. 49, no. 48, repr. in
color

Degas began fairly early in his career to use
foreground audience figures as foils for more or less
distant figures on stage. These figures seldom functioned
as traditional *repoussoirs,* but were used as silhouettes
to establish the plane of the composition. Inevitably,
the middleground was dropped away and the
background brought forward by the use of intense
colors, obvious paint or pastel application, and
complex compositional arrangements, as in this picture.
Lemoisne dates this and a related composition (Lemoisne

828) to 1885 although he assigns other similar compositions to 1878-1880 (Lemoisne 476, 577).

In 1879-1880 Mary Cassatt, who was close to Degas at the time, executed several similar pictures with the auditorium rather than the stage as a background (Breeskin 61, 62, 64, 73). There is a related Degas lithograph.

92   Edgar DEGAS (1834-1917)

Laundresses Carrying Linen
Charcoal: 17″ x 23″ (43.2 x 58.4 cm.)

Collections: Atelier Degas (4th Sale, Galerie Georges Petit, Paris, July 2-4, 1919, no. 357, repr.); Monsieur S....

Exhibitions: See catalog ref. page
First Exhibited: V
Not Exhibited: X, XX, XXIII

Literature: Sale catalog, *Collections de Monsieur S...., * Paris: Hôtel Drouot, Nov. 13, 1969, no. 20, repr. pl. III

The softness of much of this drawing suggests that it may be a re-worked counterproof, probably executed rather late in Degas' career. The figure at the right is almost identical to that in the Hammer *Laundress Carrying Linen,* but in reverse.

93   Edgar DEGAS (1834-1917)

Laundress Carrying Linen, ca. 1888-1892
Pastel: 24″ x 36 1/2″ (61.0 x 92.7 cm.)

Collection: Atelier Degas (lst sale, Paris, Galerie Georges Petit, 1918, no. 170, repr.); Durand-Ruel, Paris: Henri Fèvre, Monte Carlo; Mrs. Charles R. Henschel, New York; Lilli Wulf, New York; Irving Vogel, Philadelphia; Benjamin D. Gilbert, Stamford, Conn.

Exhibited: Paris, Galerie André Weil, *Degas, Peintre du Mouvement,* June 9-30, 1939, no. 37 (repr. p. 22)

Exhibitions: See catalog ref. page
First Exhibited: I
Not Exhibited: XX, XXIII

Literature: Sale catalog, *Catalogue des Tableaux, Pastels et Dessins par Edgar Degas,* lst sale, Paris: Galerie Georges Petit, 1918, p. 95, no. 170, repr.; P. A. Lemoisne, *Degas et son Oeuvre,* Paris: Paul Brame & C.M. de Hauke, 1947, vol. III, p. 559, no. 961, repr.

Degas returned to laundresses as a theme intermittently throughout his career. They offered him not the social

overtones one senses in Daumier's use of the same subject, but an habitual and balanced movement. His first use of the pose appearing in this pastel, which also occurs in a charcoal drawing in the Hammer Collection, was in a painting of about 1877 (Lemoisne 410) in which it was paired with a similar figure seen from the front.

This double pose was repeated at least three times about 1902, once with horses in the background (Lemoisne 1418, 1420, 1420 bis); at the same time the single figure was also repeated against a background of horses (Lemoisne 1419). There is, finally, an almost identical pastel probably close in date to this one (Lemoisne 960). In this pastel one sees how Degas could use a figure simultaneously to render volume and to create a flat pattern activating the entire surface of the composition.

94   Paul CEZANNE (1839-1906)

Study of the "Ecorché" (recto)
Pencil: 6 1/2″ x 7″ (15.9 x 17.8 cm.)
Page of Studies: The Father of the Artist (verso)
Pencil: 10 3/4″ x 7″ (27.3 x 17.8 cm.)

Collections: Sir Michael Sadler, Oxford; Leicester Galleries, London; Edward Le Bas, Brighton

Exhibited: London, Leicester Galleries, *Selection of Works from the Collection of Sir Michael Sadler,* Jan. 1944, no. 9; London, Royal Academy of Arts, *A Painter's Collection* (Edward Le Bas Coll.), Mar. 19-Apr. 28, 1963, no. 233

Exhibitions: See catalog ref. page
First Exhibited: II
Not shown: X, XX, XXIII

Literature: Sale catalog, *Impressionist and Modern Drawings, Paintings and Sculpture,* Geneva: Christie, Manson & Woods, Nov. 6, 1969, no. 154, repr.

Cézanne did a series of drawings (cf. Lionello Venturi, *Cézanne son art—son oeuvre,* Paris: Paul Rosenberg, 1936, vol. I, II, nos. 1317, 1453, 1586) and a painting (cf. Venturi no. 709) of a plaster cast. The cast was mistakenly attributed to Michelangelo in the Nineteenth Century and is called the "Ecorché." This recto is one of the drawings of this series.

95   Paul CEZANNE (1839-1906)

Mont Ste. Victoire, ca. 1895 (recto)
Watercolor: 6 7/16″ x 10 5/8″ (16.4 x 27.0 cm.)
Bed Post (verso)
Pencil and watercolor: 7 1/4″ x 10 1/4″ (18.4 x 26.0 cm.)

Collections: Leicester Galleries, London; Edward Le Bas
Brighton; Sale, Geneva, Christie, Manson & Woods
Nov. 6, 1969, no. 155, repr.

Exhibited: London, Royal Academy of Arts, *A Painter's
Collection* (Edward Le Bas Coll.), Mar. 19-Apr. 28, 1963;
no. 231; Scottish National Gallery of Modern Art, 1968; no. 231

Exhibitions: See catalog ref. page
First Exhibited: II
Not Exhibited: XX, XXIII

Literature: Sale catalog, *Impressionist and Modern Drawings,
Paintings and Sculpture,* Geneva: Christie, Manson & Woods,
Nov. 6, 1969, no. 155, repr.

**The characteristic profile of one of Cézanne's favorite
motifs is not easily discernible in this watercolor, which
emphasizes the horizontal line of trees in the middle
ground. Cézanne has used wash tones close to that of
the paper to increase the allover effect of the
composition, an effect further enhanced by the
dispersion of his accustomed broken contour.**

96 Odilon REDON (1840-1916)

Vase of Flowers
Pastel: 15 3/4″ x 12 3/8″ (40.0 x 31.4 cm.)
Signed lower right: Odilon Redon

Collection: Ruth V. McVitty, Princeton, N.J.

Exhibitions: See catalog ref. page
First Exhibited: II
Not Exhibited: XX, XXIII

Literature: François Daulte, "Hammer en dix chefs-
d'oeuvres," *Connaissance des Arts,* Sept. 1970, p. 80, repr.

**Redon's flower pieces are at once dream-like in their
disembodiment and surreal in their clarity. With no
background other than the intermediate tonality of the
bare paper, the colors in this work stand out with
unusual sharpness from each other and from the ground.
Although the ground tends to be so infinitely
atmospheric as to overwhelm the vase of flowers, the
composition is wholly convincing. One hardly notices,
for example, that the poppies or anemones are an
impossible blue.**

97 Paul GAUGUIN (1848-1903)

Landscape at Pont-Aven
Brush and ink: 12 1/2″ x 17 1/4″ (31.8 x 43.8 cm.)
Inscription lower right: No. 181

Exhibitions: See catalog ref. page
First Exhibited: II
Not Exhibited: XX, XXIII

**This outstanding drawing was executed during
Gauguin's stay in Pont-Aven, an artists' colony on the
coast of Brittany, "a land which had been little touched
by Roman civilization."**

**According to André Schoeller, the number 181 which
appears in pencil at the lower right is an indication that
the drawing was once in the possession of Emile
Schuffenecker (1851-1934), an artist who was Gauguin's
close friend for a time at Pont-Aven. He owned several
of Gauguin's drawings which were numbered in this
fashion.**

**It was in his Brittany period, from 1886 to 1890, that
Gauguin developed his style of Synthetism in which he
sought to extract from the forces of nature what they
inherently communicated to him rather than to represent
the forms of nature's outward appearance. To
accomplish this end he eschewed the traditional
"sciences" of painting in favor of his own subjective
response and interpretation. This led to a flattening out
of forms, an overriding of optical perspective, and a
use of non-naturalistic color. During these years he was
also influenced by the Art Nouveau movement as is
evident from the use of the curvilinear border which
divides the central motif of the drawing from the one
at the extreme left and gives the composition an
intriguing inner ornamental frame.**

**It seems possible to ascribe the drawing to the
period of about 1888 based on the similarity of the
house and trees with those in the painting of the same
name, dated '88, now in the collection of Stavros S.
Niarchos.**

98 Paul GAUGUIN (1848-1903)

Parau No Te Varau Ino (left)
Tahitian Legend (right)
Pen, brush, and India ink; two drawings on one sheet, side by
side: 6″ x 3 1/2″ (15.2 x 8.9 cm.)

Collections: Galerie Druet, Paris; Sale, London, Sotheby &
Co., Apr. 16, 1970, no. 49, p. 39, repr. opp.

Exhibitions: See catalog ref. page
First Exhibited: IV
Not Exhibited: X, XX, XXIII

Literature: John Rewald, *Paul Gauguin,* New York, London,
and Paris: Hyperion Press, 1938 and 1949; Sale catalog,
Impressionist and Modern Drawings and Watercolors,
London: Sotheby & Co., Apr. 16, 1970, no. 49, p. 39, repr.
opp.

The drawing on the left is the reverse of the woodcut *Eve* by Gauguin (Guérin 57), and it is not improbable that it is a preliminary model for the print. The woodcut was printed in an edition of thirty.

Guérin states that in the original manuscript of *Noa Noa*, Gauguin attached a photograph of a drawing representing the same figures which appear in the woodcut, but in reversed positions. The Hammer sketch may have been the one described.

Parau No Te Varau Ino is a study for the painting of the same title, meaning "words of the Devil," in the collection of Ambassador and Mrs. Averell Harriman, New York (Wildenstein no. 458).

The support of the two Hammer studies is heavy wove J. Whatman paper. Their borders indicate that they were undoubtedly intended for prints.

99   Paul GAUGUIN (1848-1903)

Tahitian Heads
Page from Gauguin's *Tahiti Sketchbook*
Pencil: 6 3/4″ x 4″ (16.2 x 10.2 cm.)

Collections: Dr. Warner Muensterberger, New York: Robert Q. Lewis, Los Angeles

Exhibitions: See catalog ref. page
First Exhibited: II
Not Exhibited: X, XX, XXIII

Literature: Bernard Dorival (ed.), *Paul Gauguin, Carnet de Tahiti*, Paris: Quatre Chemins, 1954, no. 85

100   Paul GAUGUIN (1848-1903)

Pages from Sketchbook No. 16
Page size 6 1/2″ x 4 1/4″ (16.5 x 10.8 cm.)

Collection: Henri Mahaut (purchased in Cherbourg)

Exhibitions: See catalog ref. page
First Exhibited: II
Not Exhibited: X, XX, XXIII

Literature: Henri Mahaut, "Notes Synthétiques par Gauguin"; *Vers et Prose*, July-Sept. 1910; John Rewald, *Gauguin*, Paris: Hyperion, 1938, boy with goose repr. p. 9; boy with pail repr. p. 8; Raymond Cogniat and John Rewald, *Paul Gauguin, a Sketchbook*, New York: Hammer Galleries, 1962 (facsimile reprint of Sketchbook No. 16, publication and translation of "Notes Synthétiques" and critical notes)

100-A   *Breton Peasant*
Pencil and crayon
Page 18 in Sketchbook

100-B   *Little Breton Boy*
Pencil and crayon
Page 19 in Sketchbook
Executed in Brittany in 1888. The same boy appears in *The Swineherd* (repr. in Georges Wildenstein, *Gauguin,* Paris: Les Beaux-Arts, 1964, vol. I, no. 255), now in the Norton Simon Collection, Los Angeles, and the *The Little Breton Shepherd* (Wildenstein, op. cit. no. 256)

100-C   *Little Breton Boy*
Pencil and crayon
Page 20 in Sketchbook
The same boy as in 100 B

100-D   *Bridge at Pont-Aven (?)*
Pencil and crayon
Page 26 in Sketchbook

100-E   *Two Breton Women*
Pencil and crayon
Page 29 in Sketchbook

100-F   *Head and Hand of a Monkey*
Pencil and crayon
Page 36 in Sketchbook

100-G   *Little Breton Boy with Goose*
Pencil and crayon
Page 37 in Sketchbook
The same boy as in 100 B and C

100-H   *Little Breton Boy with Pail*
Pencil and crayon
Page 38 in Sketchbook
The same boy as in 100 B, C and G

100-I   *Little Breton Boy with Pail*
Pencil and crayon
Page 39 in Sketchbook
The same boy as in 100 B, C, G and H

100-J   *Sketches of a Child*
Ink
Page 79 in Sketchbook
Cogniat (see Literature above) remarks that this child is not a peasant, but is reminiscent of the children in the artist's own family and in that of his Danish wife

100-K *Landscape*
Ink
Page 81 in Sketchbook

100-L *Head of a Child and Self-Portrait*
Ink
Page 86 in Sketchbook
Head of child prepared for enlargement
Inscribed: Gauguin par lui-même

100-M *Head of Child and Head of Man* (probably self-portrait)
Ink
Page 87 in Sketchbook

100-N *Profile of Woman and Profile of Boy*
Ink
Page 95 in Sketchbook

100-O *Head of Woman, Tree, and Head of Man*
Ink
Page 96 in Sketchbook
Cogniat (see Literature above) remarks that the woman may
be an Arlésienne.

100-P *Self-Portrait*
Pencil
Page 111 in Sketchbook
Reminiscent of the 1885 painting, *Before the Easel,* in the
collection of Dr. Jacques Koerfer, Bern (Wildenstein, op. cit
no. 138)

101   Pierre-Auguste RENOIR (1841-1919)

Girlhood
Pencil: 13 3/8″ x 11 3/8″ (34.0 x 28.9 cm.)
Signed upper right: Renoir

Collection: Mrs. William Wilson, New York

Exhibited: Paris, Galerie Charpentier, 1949, no. 282 bis

Exhibitions: See catalog ref. page
First Exhibited: II
Not Exhibited: X, XX, XXIII

Literature: *L'Exposition au Profit des Pauvres de la
Fédération Nationale des Fils des Morts pour La France,*
Paris: Galerie Charpentier, 1949, no. 282 bis

———————————

**This drawing served Renoir as the model for his
drypoint *Sur la plage, à Berneval* (1892?) which Loys
Delteil also used as the frontispiece for his catalog of
the artist's prints in volume sixteen of *Le Peintre-***

Graveur Illustré. **According to Delteil, there are three
states of the print. It is the last state, after the beveling
of the plate, which is reproduced in his catalog.**

  **The placement of the two girls is reversed in the
print: they face towards the middle right. Figures of
bathers have been added in the background.**

  **When the third state of the print was sold at the G.
Pochet sale in 1902, it was entitled *Aux Bains de Mer.***

102   Vincent VAN GOGH (1853-1890)

The Zandmennik House, ca. (1879-1880)
Charcoal: 9″ x 11 3/4″ (22.9 x 29.8 cm.)
Signed with initials: V.G.

Collections: Decrucq, Cuesmes; M. G. Delsaut, Cuesmes;
Samuel Delsaut, Cuesmes, 1960

Exhibited: Paris, Musée Jacquemart-André, *Vincent van Gogh,*
Feb.-Mar. 1960, no. 200, p. 56; Cuesmes, Borinage, *Vincent van
Gogh,* Oct. 1-20, 1960, no. 8

Exhibitions: See catalog ref. page
First Exhibited: IV
Not Exhibited: X, XX, XXIII

Literature: Amsterdam, Stedelijk Museum, *Museum Journaal,*
series 5, no. 4, Oct. 1959, pp. 80-81, repr.; M. E. Tralbaut,
Le Mal Aimé, Lausanne: 1969, p. 63; J. B. de la Faille, *The
Works of Vincent van Gogh, His Paintings and Drawings,*
Amsterdam: Meulenhoff International, New York: Reynal &
Co., with William Morrow & Co., Inc., 1970, no. XXXIII,
p. 609; Sale catalog, *Impressionist and Modern Drawings,
Paintings and Sculpture,* London: Christie, Manson & Woods,
Apr. 14, 1970, no. 42, p. 34, repr. opp.

103   Vincent VAN GOGH (1853-1890)

The Magrot House, Cuesmes, ca. 1879-1880
Charcoal 9″ x 11 3/4″ (22.9 x 29.8 cm.)
Signed with initials: V.G.

Collections: Decrucq, Cuesmes; M. G. Delsaut, Cuesmes;
Samuel Delsaut, Cuesmes

Exhibited: Paris, Musée Jacquemart-André, *Vincent van Gogh,*
Feb.-Mar. 1960, no. 199, p. 56; Cuesmes, Borinage, *Vincent van
Gogh,* Oct. 1-20, 1960, no. 9

Exhibitions: See catalog ref. page
First Exhibited: IV
Not Exhibited: X, XX, XXIII

Literature: *Museum Journaal,* series 5, no. 4, Amsterdam:
Stedelijk Museum, Oct. 1959, pp. 80-81, repr.; M. E. Tralbaut,

Le Mal Aimé, Lausanne: 1969, p. 63; J. B. de la Faille, *The Works of Vincent van Gogh, His Paintings and Drawings,* Amsterdam: Meulenhoff International, New York: Reynal & Co., with William Morris & Co., Inc., 1970, XXXII, p. 609; Sale catalog: *Impressionist and Modern Drawings, Paintings and Sculpture,* London: Christie, Manson & Woods, Apr. 14, 1970, no. 41, p. 34, repr. opp.

104   Vincent VAN GOGH (1853-1890)

Old Man Carrying a Bucket, 1882
Pencil heightened with gray and black wash
18 3/4″ x 8 1/4″ (47.6 x 21.0 cm.)

Collections: Ubbergen, The Netherlands; H. C. Stork, Vienna; W. P. Maclaine Pont, Bilthoven; Mrs. A. W. Maclaine Pont-Stork, Zwolle; J. Donna, The Hague

Exhibitions: See catalog ref. page
First Exhibited: VI
Not Exhibited: X, XX, XXIII

Literature: *The Letters of Vincent van Gogh to His Brother,* London: Constable & Co., Ltd., 1927, vol. II, Letter 251 (Dec. 4-9), pp. 40-46; J. B. de la Faille, *L'Oeuvre de Vincent van Gogh, Catalogue Raisonné,* Paris and Brussels: Les Editions G. van Oest, 1928, vol. III, no. 964, p. 33 vol. IV, pl. XXXV; Dr. Walther Vanbeselaere, *De Hollandsche Periode (1880-1885) in Het Werk van Vincent van Gogh,* Antwerp: De Sikkel, 1937, pp. 97, 170, 208, 409; *The Complete Letters of Vincent van Gogh* (preface Vincent W. van Gogh, ed. Mrs. J. van Gogh-Bonger), Greenwich, Conn.: New York Graphic Society, 1958; Letter 251, pp. 504-508; J. B. de la Faille, *The Works of Vincent van Gogh, His Paintings and Drawings,* Amsterdam: Meulenhoff International, New York: Reynal & Co., with William Morrow & Co., 1970, no. F964, pp. 360, 648, repr. p. 360; Sale catalog, *Impressionist and Modern Watercolours, Drawings and Bronzes,* London: Sotheby & Co., July 2, 1970, no. 20, p. 35, repr. opp. and cat. cover

105   Vincent VAN GOGH (1853-1890)

Man Polishing a Boot, 1882
Black chalk, pencil heightened with white and gray wash
19″ x 10 1/2″ (48.3 x 26.7 cm.)

Collections: H. P. Bremmer, The Hague; Heirs of H. P. Bremmer, The Hague; E. J. van Wisselingh & Co., Amsterdam; Mrs. J. G. ter Kuile-ter Kuile, Switzerland; Sale, New York, Christie, Manson & Woods, Apr. 6, 1970, no. 61, p. 46, repr. opp.

Exhibited: Amsterdam, E. J. van Wisselingh & Co., *Vincent van Gogh, Aquarelles et Dessins de l'Epoque 1881-1885, Provenant*

de Collections Particulieres Néerlandaises, April 19-May 18, 1961, no. 19, repr.

Exhibitions: See catalog ref. page
First Exhibited: IV
Not Exhibited: X, XXIII

Literature: *The Letters of Vincent van Gogh to His Brother,* London: Constable & Co., Ltd. 1927, Letter 235: pp. 530-533, Letter 236: pp. 533-535; Letter 238: pp. 539-543; J. B. de la Faille, *L'Oeuvre de Vincent van Gogh, Catalogue Raisonné,* Paris and Brussels: Editions G. van Oest, 1928, vol. III, no. 969, vol. IV, pl. XXXVII; Dr. Walter Vanbeselaere, *Der Hollandsche Periode (1880-1885) in Het Werk van Vincent van Gogh,* Antwerp: De Sikkel, 1937, pp. 88, 91, 170, 190, 409; *Letters to an Artist: from Vincent van Gogh to Anton ridder van Rappard, 1881-1885* (trans. Rela van Messel, intro. Walter Pach), New York: Viking Press, 1937, p. 48; *Letters de van Gogh à van Rappard* (trans. L. Roelandt), Paris: Bernard Grasset, 1950; *The Complete Letters of Vincent van Gogh* (preface Vincent W. van Gogh, ed. Mrs. J. van Gogh-Bonger), Greenwich, Conn: New York Graphic Society, 1958, Letter 235: pp. 463-466; Letter 236: pp. 466-467; Letter 238: pp. 470-473; J. B. de la Faille, *The Works of Vincent van Gogh, His Paintings and Drawings,* Amsterdam: Meulenhoff International, New York: Reynal & Co. with William Morrow & Co., Inc., 1970, no. F969, pp. 361, 648, repr. p. 361; Sale catalog, *Impressionist, American and Modern Paintings and Watercolors,* Houston, Texas: Christie, Manson & Woods (New York), Apr. 6, 1970, no. 61, p. 46, repr. opp.

_____

A great artist's student or formative work, when present, is always pertinent as a means of assessing the magnitude of his development, and very rarely has that development been as marked as in the case of van Gogh's drawing style.

The two Hammer Collection studies of cottages date from 1879-1880; the two studies of workers date from The Hague period, December 1881 to September 1883. The four thus show van Gogh's early works, from his twenty-sixth to his thirtieth year. Homely, primitive, "amateurish," they are among his first earnest efforts to portray the poor and humble—old men at their daily tasks and simple cottages of country folk—and they furnish a revealing contrast to his subsequent progress.

Within the next two years van Gogh advanced to a remarkable level of drawing which went far beyond his first stiff and crude essays. The hard, rude lines and general awkwardness gave way to a powerful command of *graphisme,* particularly in his peasant studies. His modeling became free, bold, and decisive, his forms broad and monumental. Van Gogh's vigorous treatment of the laboring figure in all of its tension far surpassed

the treatment of similar subjects in the drawings of Millet, who had been one of his central inspirations.

106 Henri-Edmond CROSS (1856-1910)

Cypresses, 1896
Gouache: 9 1/2 " x 13 1/4" (24.1 x 33.7 cm.)

Collections: William J. Holliday, Indianapolis; Modern Art Foundation, Geneva; Pierre Matisse Gallery, New York

Exhibited: Cleveland, Ohio, Cleveland Museum of Art, *Tenth Exhibition of Watercolors and Pastels,* Jan. 10-Feb. 12, 1933

Exhibitions: See catalog ref. page
First Exhibited: II
Not Exhibited: X, XX, XXIII

Literature: Isabelle Compin, *H. E. Cross,* Paris: Quatre Chemins, 1964, repr. pp. 146, 338

Miss Compin reproduces an oil, 25 1/2" x 36 1/4", of the identical image, entitled *Nocturne,* painted in 1896 and now in the collection of M. O. Ghez, Geneva. She also reproduces a four-color lithograph, 11 1/8" x 16 1/8", published by Vollard in 1896 as *La Promenade.* Miss Compin believes she may have found the source of the subject in a play of 1891 by Edouard Dujardin. In the play, *Le Chevalier Passé,* Act III, Scene I, night is falling and the four Floramyes, preparing to leave the isle of Antonia, lament: "Adieu, les rives où nous avons vécu! Adieu, les charmants bords où nos songes longtemps ne sont plus!"

107 Georges SEURAT (1859-1891)

Study after 'The Models,' 1888
Pen and ink: 10 1/16" x 6 3/8" (26.0 x 16.5 cm.)
Signed lower left: Seurat

Collections: Emile Seurat, Paris; Alexandre Natanson, Paris; Galerie Bolette Natanson, Paris; Jean-Charles Moreux, Paris; Mme. Jean-Charles Moreux, Paris; Wildenstein & Co., Inc., New York; Norton Simon, Los Angeles

Exhibited: Paris, La Revue Blanche, *Seurat,* Mar. 19-Apr. 5, 1900 (hors. cat.); Paris, Galerie Bernheim-Jeune, *Rétrospective Georges Seurat,* Dec. 14, 1908-Jan. 9, 1909, no. 197; Paris, Galerie Bernheim-Jeune, *Les Dessins de Seurat,* Nov. 29-Dec. 24, 1926, no. 114; London, Galerie Syrie Maugham, Bolette Natanson, *Seurat,* May 21-June 7, 1935; Paris, Galerie Paul Rosenberg, *Georges Seurat,* Feb. 3-29, 1936, no. 130, suppl.; Paris, Galerie Bolette Natanson, "Les

Cadres," *Peintres de la Revue Blanche,* 1936, no. 50, suppl.; Paris, Musée Jacquemart-André, *Seurat,* Nov.-Dec. 1957, no. 55

Exhibitions: See catalog ref. page
First Exhibited: IX
Not Exhibited: X, XX, XXIII
Exhibited: Washington, D.C., National Gallery of Art, National Gallery Exhibition, June 2-September 1, 1974

Literature: Paul Adam, "Les Impressionistes à l'Exposition des Indépendants," *La Vie Moderne,* Paris, Apr. 15, 1888, p. 229, repr.; André Lhote, *Georges Seurat,* Rome: Editions de Valori Plastici, Coll. "Les Artistes Nouveaux," 1922, p. II, repr.; Florent Fels, "Les Dessins de Georges Seurat," *L'Amour de l'Art,* no. I, Paris, Jan. 1927, p. 43, repr.; Gustave Kahn, *Les Dessins de Georges Seurat,* Paris: Editions Bernheim-Jeune, 1928, pl. 98, repr.; Waldemar George, *Seurat et le Divisionnisme,* Paris: Editions Librairie de France, Coll. "Les Albums d'Art Druet," 1928, p. 15, repr.; Thadée Natanson, "Sur Une Exposition des Peintres de la Revue Blanche," *Arts et Métiers Graphiques,* no. 54, Paris, Aug. 15, 1936, p. 16, repr.; Robert J. Goldwater, "Some Aspects of the Development of Seurat's Style," *The Art Bulletin,* vol. XXIII, no. 2, New York: Wittenborn & Co., 1946, no. 80, p. 104, repr.; Henri Dorra and John Rewald, *Seurat, L'Oeuvre Peint, Biographie et Catalogue Critique,* Paris: Les Beaux-Arts, Editions d'Etudes et de Documents, 1959, no. 179a, p. 222, repr.; C. M. de Hauke, *Seurat et Son Oeuvre,* Paris: Gründ, 1961, vol. II, no. 665, p. 254, repr.; Sale catalog, *Highly Important 19th and 20th Century Paintings, Drawings and Sculpture, from the Private Collection of Norton Simon,* New York: Parke-Bernet Galleries, Inc., May 5, 1971, no. 46, p. 88, repr. opp.

According to Dorra-Rewald, this is a copy made by the artist after the central figure in his painting, *The Models.* Created to serve as an illustration for the review, *La Vie Moderne,* it appeared in the issue of April 15, 1888.

Seurat was rarely active as an illustrator or poster artist. He is known to have provided a cover for a novel by Victor Jose, a writer for whose works Toulouse-Lautrec executed several posters.

To be noted in this line drawing is the complete alteration of the expression of the original model's face.

108 Pierre BONNARD (1867-1947)

Girl Drying Her Knees
Pencil: 13" x 9 1/2" (33.0 x 24.1 cm.)
Signed lower right: Bonnard

109   Pablo PICASSO (1881-1973)

Female Nude (recto)
Pencil: 6 1/2″ x 4″ (16.5 x 10.2 cm.)
Signed upper right: Picasso
Young Man, ca. 1906 (verso)
Pen and ink: 6 1/2″ x 4″ (16.5 x 10.2 cm.)
Signed lower right: Picasso

Collections: Saidenberg Gallery, New York; George Axelrod,
New York

Exhibitions: See catalog ref. page
First Exhibited: IV
Not Exhibited: X, XX, XXIII

Literature: Sale Catalog, *Impressionists and Modern Drawing
and Watercolors,* London: Sotheby & Co., Apr. 16, 1970, no.
92, pp. 118-119, repr.

———————————

**This double-sided drawing belongs to the period of
1906, and the female nude incorporates many of the
"classicizing" features which Picasso adopted at that
time. His work became simplified, more abstract and
sculptural. The face with its far-off gaze is delineated
with a minimum of lines and accords with various other
"mask-like" portraits of the period. But the relatively
broad, squat body, treated in summary fashion, reflects
some of the quality of the late Iberian sculpture which
was another factor in Picasso's earlier work.**

**That the verso sketch is so close to being a caricature
suggests that it may have been drawn of a friend, perhaps
at a cafe. An earlier sketch of roughly the same type, in
which the man leans his arm on a cafe table, was formerly
in the Galerie Rosengart in Lucerne, Switzerland.**

Index of Artists